Navigating the Politics of Healthcare

Navigating the Politics of Healthcare

A Compliance Officer's Guide to Communication, Relationships, and Gaining Buy-in

Jay Anstine

PALMETTO
PUBLISHING

Charleston, SC
www.PalmettoPublishing.com

Navigating the Politics of Healthcare

Cover image by Jacek Sopotnicki at Sopotnicki Photography
www.sopotnicki.com

First Edition

Hardcover ISBN: 979-8-8229-0248-0
Paperback ISBN: 979-8-8229-0249-7
eBook ISBN: 979-8-8229-0250-3

To McKenzie, Rubie, and Hill,
you are my purpose in life.

Contents

My Story

Like some other healthcare compliance professionals, I fell into this line of work. Maybe a day will come when a seven-year-old says, "Gee, Dad, I want to be a compliance officer when I grow up." For me, that was not the case. At that age, I had my sights set on a very stable career—professional golf.

When I was in college, I majored in political science at Montana State University in Bozeman, Montana. At the time, I discovered that I enjoyed reading, writing, and learning about our government. Never was there a thought of running for office. Also, my grades from my freshman year math and science courses were horrifying, so I knew that jobs like chemical engineer, architect, rocket scientist...yeah, they were not going to be in my future. I am an avid skier too, so my degree choice, one requiring an occasional paper, was also conducive to unexpected powder days. You've got to have priorities in life, right?

Kidding aside, during my time in college, I did identify a natural interest in the rule of law. It can be traced back to my major, but also an internship I had with a local judge in Bozeman. My junior year, I had made a promise to myself that one day I would go on to law school. Despite making that promise, I decided that after graduation, I needed some time away from school. Time to explore other career opportunities, including one that, funny enough, did involve a short stint in professional golf.

After bouncing around in a few different jobs, I eventually applied for and was offered a job in healthcare. I worked in provider relations for a managed care organization that was part of a nonprofit health system. From that experience, I discovered that I also had a natural interest in healthcare. I loved the fact that patients were ultimately the customer. It made me feel connected to a greater good.

After a couple of years working in healthcare, it was starting to feel like law school was slipping away. One particular day, I was sitting in my cubicle, kind of down, thinking "Are we doing this or not? It's now or never." So, I chose "now." That night, I picked up some study guides for the law school entrance exam (LSAT), took the test, and thankfully got accepted into school. By this point, it had been five years since graduating from college, but I fulfilled the promise that I made to myself.

When I entered law school, my thought was to somehow marry these two natural interests. I thought "Well. People will always need healthcare, and they'll always need lawyers. It's not professional golf, but hey, this seems like job security to me." So off I went for three years to learn about things like personal jurisdiction, strict scrutiny, and res judicata.[1]

After graduating from law school, I worked for a couple of years for the general counsel of the same health system I

---

1 *Personal Jurisdiction* is a concept covered in fist year Civil Procedure courses and refers to the power a court has to make a decision related to a party in a case. *Strict Scrutiny* is a recognized form of judicial review of a law to determine constitutionality. It is covered in first year Constitutional Law courses. *Res Judicata* is a legal doctrine recognized by courts. It is also covered in first year Civil Procedure and provides that a legal claim against a party cannot be relitigated once it has been judged on its merits.

had worked for before school. At the time, I was focused on practicing law as a career, but a couple life events simultaneously occurred that altered my career path. The first was that my position in the general counsel's office came to an end due to budget cuts. The second was the end of a long-term relationship. Clearly, I was living my best life at the time. Joking aside, my girlfriend was pursuing a graduate degree out of state and we were just drifting apart in life.

So, these events put me in a position of having to decide whether I was going to continue to pursue practicing law and whether I was going to remain in my hometown. Since my hometown was relatively small at the time and my interest was very specific, there weren't a lot of opportunities there to practice healthcare law. Having grown up as a ski racer, the mountains have always been in my heart, and so my focus shifted to relocating back to a place where my heart belonged. This time it would be Colorado. As I was looking for work, I discovered there were more available compliance positions than legal positions. This opened my eyes for the first time to healthcare compliance. After applying for countless positions, I eventually landed one in Denver.

After a year or so working as a compliance specialist, it became evident to me that compliance was a better fit to sustain my interest. Since the work was connected to things like conducting investigations, educating staff, and responding to regulatory changes, every day seemed like an opportunity to learn something new. I liked that. I also spent several years reviewing and drafting legal documents in an in-house counsel's office, so I knew what *that* work was like. I knew of the time required to produce a contract or other legal document, the volume of demands from leadership, and the lack of staffing to keep up with the demands. These factors all seemed like a road to burn out for me if I stayed on that course.

What I have found interesting about my career choice, in a laugh-at-myself way, is the fact that when I was in college, I had absolutely zero ambitions of *ever* being a politician. But now here I am, looking back over a career spanning more than twenty years that has required me to play politician almost on a daily basis.

To me, the most challenging part of our work is managing the business relationship. In an odd way, it's also the part of the job I've found the most mentally stimulating. For that reason, I started speaking at local and national conferences on many of the topics that became part of this book. The reason I wrote this book is that after my presentations, I would have chief compliance officers coming up to me, expressing appreciation for the topics. They were telling me the information was so needed for their newer compliance officers. If that is you, then this book is for you. I hope you enjoy reading it as much as I did writing it.

Introduction

From scheduling patients to delivering care to reimbursement, healthcare is an industry functioning on a daily basis under a mountain of federal, state, and local regulations in the United States. To help navigate this mountain, many healthcare organizations have adopted corporate compliance programs ("compliance programs"). During the 1990s, the federal government strongly encouraged the voluntary adoption of such programs for healthcare organizations participating in Medicare and Medicaid.[1] The rationale behind the government's position was that such efforts will help reduce fraud, waste, and abuse in these taxpayer-funded programs.

To assist healthcare organizations, the Department of Health and Human Services, Office of Inspector General (OIG) issued guidelines for several subsections of the healthcare industry. Commonly referred to as a CPG, these guidelines set forth certain components of a compliance program. As you can imagine, reading through a CPG is about as exhilarating as reading through a phone book. (Do we even have phone books anymore?) Nonetheless, these components have become known in the compliance profession as the "Seven Elements." They represent what the federal government considers to be key fundamental aspects of an effective compliance program. One of the Seven Elements relates to the appointment of a compliance officer, which is the focal point of this book.

In 2010, there was a notable shift in the government's viewpoint of compliance programs when the Patient Protection and Affordable Care Act of 2010 (PPACA) was signed into law. For the first time, the adoption of compliance programs became mandatory for healthcare organizations participating in Medicare and Medicaid.[2] Since then, compliance programs have increasingly become an essential part of any healthcare organization's operations. In today's highly regulated healthcare environment, compliance programs aid in identifying and responding to regulatory risk to avoid, or reduce, an organization's corporate liability.

A common reality to the compliance officer profession is the fact that the business of healthcare is political. To be clear, when I say the business of healthcare is political, I'm not referring to the politicization of healthcare (i.e., healthcare being argued as a right or privilege). Instead, I am talking about the industry's business environment—more specifically, the individuals working inside the industry and their various self-interests. As we will explore in this book, there are a number of key individuals a compliance officer works with on a daily basis. This list includes healthcare executives, physicians, administrative and clinical workers, government agencies, third-party contractors, as well as patients and their families.

As with any self-interest, there will be times when they align with the organization's compliance program, and times when, well…they will not. If you have ever advised a leader not to engage in certain conduct, only to find out he or she did it anyway, then you know what I mean. If you have ever been uninvited to an operations meeting to discuss a new venture ("Whoops. Did I do that?"), then you know what I mean. If you have ever walked into a room and the conversation awkwardly pauses or shifts to a new topic, then you know what I mean. The good news is that (a) you're not alone, and (b) this book will help you.

The pages that follow are dedicated to outlining steps a compliance officer can take to navigate these self-interests and become more politically adept in the organization. While not a compliance program element per se, becoming politically adept will help you carry out each of the Seven Elements more effectively. After orienting to the politics of healthcare, the discussion will cover some key strategies you can put into action, such as building strong relationships with leaders, using diplomacy to communicate and resolve issues, and establishing and maintaining healthy boundaries.

The content of this book has been written primarily for new compliance officers or individuals on a career path to becoming one. Separately, noncompliance folks, such as healthcare leaders, may also find it helpful in defining an ideal compliance officer for their organization. Just keep in mind that because the primary audience is new compliance officers, it has been written to assume the reader has no regulatory or operational experience in healthcare.

Throughout this book, I will refer to "healthcare organizations." This reference is broadly intended to cover organizations on the provider and payer side of the industry; the ones directly or indirectly providing services reimbursable by a federal healthcare program (e.g., Medicare and Medicaid). In the eyes of the federal government, these are the types of organizations that must have compliance programs in place.

A significant challenge to becoming proficient as a compliance officer is experience. Fortunately or unfortunately, that means enduring a heavy dose of trial and error. If you have ever fumbled through changing a flat tire for the first time without guidance, then you know what I mean. ("Is the first step to loosen the tire's lug nuts, or raise up the car?") When it comes to the daily work of a compliance officer, there is an endless list of new-to-you political experiences you'll encounter. While it'd be impossible to assemble a compilation of every experience, this book is intended to cover the common ones we all face at some point in our careers. By taking this approach, I wanted to provide guidance as if I were standing on the side of the road with you. (By the way, if you didn't know, you loosen the lug nuts first.)

Over the course of my career, I have seen my fair share of messes based on the politics of healthcare, and I've even created some myself. Throughout this book, I will share some stories of struggles. Lots of struggles. My intent in taking this approach is twofold. First, to illustrate how easily one can unknowingly get pulled into a political mess. Second, to provide you with lessons learned from these struggles to help you avoid the same mistakes I and others have made. For these reasons, the overall goal of this book is to help you in reducing some of the learning curve associated with this profession.

Finally, this book has been written with the intention of being a conversation and not a lecture. Assume that you were a new compliance officer, and you reached out to pick my brain about the realities of your new career choice. If we were sitting in a coffee shop or having lunch, the pages that follow would make up our time together. So seek out your favorite coffee shop or lunch spot, put in your order, and let's let the conversation begin.

Chapter One

The Politics of Healthcare

Commerce with all Nations, alliance with none, should be our motto.
—Thomas Jefferson

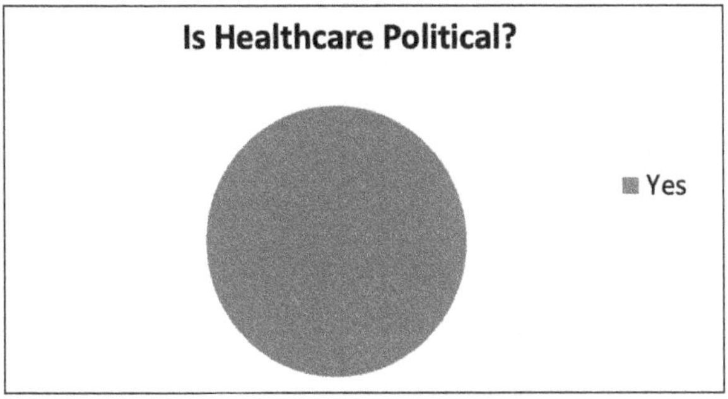

When I think back on my life before my career, I had no idea there was a whole other world that existed in healthcare unknown to the general public. A world where physicians fight with each other over patients. A world where hospitals fight with physicians over compensation. A world where healthcare workers fight with each other over workflow issues impacting patient care. And a world where everyone is fighting the government over increasing bureaucracy and decreasing reimbursement.

It is this "other world" where you find the politics of healthcare alive, impacting how care is delivered. For you, the compliance officer, it impacts how you operate the compliance program. More specifically, it affects how you advise healthcare leaders on proposed business deals. It affects how you educate staff on regulatory or policy requirements. It affects how you conduct investigations, perform audits, and implement corrective action. There is no element of a compliance program immune to the politics of healthcare.

Why Is Healthcare Political?

Like any industry, healthcare organizations are run by human beings. As humans, we all show up for work with our own set of opinions, emotions, and self-interests. We are also social creatures who develop and maintain relationships. These relationships become complex—and therefore political—when we are put in a position to compete with each other for time, attention, and limited resources. Healthcare is also political because of individual goals (personal or professional). Throughout the organization, operational decisions are made as a result of advancing *someone's* goals. Finally, the business of healthcare, like other industries, is political because of power, either of those who hold the power to make decisions or those who hold the power *to influence* those who make decisions. For example, a CEO sitting atop the organizational chart is going to hold more power than others in the organization to make decisions. That's formal power. Separately, there may be others in the organization, such as a vice president, a department director, or even the administrative assistant, who have the ability to influence the CEO in making decisions. That's informal power. If you want to navigate the politics of healthcare successfully, always be mindful of who holds formal and informal power.

Like workers in any other industry, healthcare workers play political games in order to get what they want. For example, let's say a group of orthopedic physicians want more control over a hospital's orthopedic service line. They want an increased ability to make operational decisions in how care is provided. Oh, and they also want a larger portion of the reimbursement from payers. A political game these docs might play would be to lobby the hospital CEO to partner with them in building a new facility together. If negotiations fail, their backup position may be threatening to compete with the hospital if their demands are not met.

Driven by promoting their own self-interests, healthcare workers find ways to align themselves with others who hold power in the organization (formally or informally). They'll hold secret meetings to discuss and negotiate deals, just like politicians in Washington, D.C. Whether it is senior management, physicians, employees, or patients, each group has a viewpoint on how the organization should conduct its business.

My first exposure to the politics of healthcare came when I was working as a compliance officer for a medium-size health system. I got pulled into a situation involving a hospital CEO who was wanting to give a gift to a group of physicians on the medical staff. If you're not familiar, there is a federal law, generally known as the Stark law, that prohibits physicians from making referrals of certain healthcare services to an entity the physician (or an immediate family member of the physician) has a financial relationship with, unless an exception applies.[3] Without boring you with the details of the Stark law, just note there is an exception (called nonmonetary compensation). This exception allows hospitals to provide certain gifts to physicians, up to an annual monetary limit.[4] An example of the type of gift I'm talking about would be a fruit basket a hospital sends out to all referring physicians around the holidays to thank them for their business.

As it relates to the question at hand, the gift itself was an electronic device, which was intended to thank the physicians who had attended the hospital's medical staff retreat. The electronic device itself and the intent of the gift were not issues. It was the fact that the gift exceeded the annual dollar limit at the time. Based on the circumstances, there was not another available exception under Stark to allow for the gift.

Political games surfaced after the CEO was told not to give the gift because it exceeded the annual dollar limit. Alternative gift suggestions were also offered by the compliance department. Instead of following our advice, the CEO went ahead and purchased the gifts anyway. Why? Because relationships with some of the physicians were strained, and the CEO was attempting to win them back. Eventually the CEO was convinced to offer another gift of lesser value—but not before more political games were played. There were attempts to convince the legal department to provide the gift. There were also attempts to convince some members of health system's senior management that providing the gift was acceptable. And of course, throughout all these lobbying efforts, the compliance department was cast as the villain for not allowing the original gift to go forward.

While the issue ultimately was resolved, the experience became a pivotal learning moment for me early in my career. I quickly realized that healthcare organizations are political entities in and of themselves, much like Congress. I learned how operational decisions could become political, and that healthcare workers will exhaust endless amounts of time and energy to cut deals when they don't get when they want. Most importantly, I learned that compliance officers can get caught up in the middle of these political games. Say the "wrong thing" and it will get used against you. From this experience, I knew that if I wanted to succeed in this profession, I needed to know how the political game is played.

The Tale of Two Agendas

For any healthcare organization, there are two agendas: the business agenda and the compliance program agenda. As the compliance officer, you will find that these two agendas serve as the platforms supporting the political games played around you.

The organization's business agenda relates to the operational and financial goals of the organization. What new service lines do we want to capture in our market? How many days do we have available cash-on-hand? What does our patient volume look like? What is our payer mix? What percentage of insurance denials are we successfully overturning? These are just some of the aspects of the organization's business agenda. If the organization provides care to patients, then providing high-quality and safe care is also part of that agenda. The organization's business agenda lies in the background of many, if not all, of the decisions that healthcare leaders make every day. For that reason, many political games played by healthcare workers relate to advancing this agenda.

Separate from an organization's business agenda is the compliance program's agenda. Generally speaking, ensuring the organization and its workforce remain in compliance with all federal, state, and local laws and regulations *is* the compliance program's agenda. More specifically, conducting investigations in response to identified issues is part of that agenda. Advising healthcare leaders regarding proposed business deals is part of that agenda. And promoting an organizational culture of compliance that encourages ethical conduct is part of that agenda. While not an all-inclusive list, these are representative of activities that support the organization's compliance program agenda. As we will explore later on in this book, there are times when these agendas are aligned and times when they conflict.

The success of your program will be dependent upon frequent times when you'll have to broker a negotiation with your leaders to keep these agendas aligned. These moments will become the times you need to know how the political game is played. Some of these moments will be easy, while others will test your ability to remain professional and committed to your career.

Quick Tip: Tale of Two Agendas

Understand the Business Side of Your Organization. Take time to know your organization's business agenda. Having this knowledge will help you relate to your healthcare leaders and understand *the why* behind the decisions they make.

Bonus Material: Need help thinking about what topics to address in order to understand the business side of your organization? If so, you can find a sample of questions to consider at http://www.bluebirdhealthlaw.com/book-bonuses.

Where Does Compliance Fit into the Politics of Healthcare?

You may have noted the quotation from Thomas Jefferson at the beginning of this chapter: "Commerce with all Nations, alliance with none should be our motto." Several years ago I stumbled upon that quotation while preparing for a conference presentation. I think it perfectly illustrates the role we have to play when it comes to the politics of healthcare. Another way to think of our role is to think of the compliance department as Switzerland within your organization. For many centuries, Switzerland has held to a policy of armed neutrality when it comes to global affairs. Like Switzerland, when it comes to the four walls of the organization, compliance officers have to be neutral when interacting with others. In reality, that means being independent and objective (i.e., nonjudgmental) in how you approach your work. To successfully navigate the politics of healthcare, you cannot play favorites with any particular individual or department. If you do, your ability to remain independent and objective will be questioned, and relatedly, your work may be viewed as flawed. So how do you maintain a neutral position within the organization? By developing a political strategy focused on productive politics.

Developing a Neutral Political Strategy

When it comes to the politics of healthcare, you want to develop a political strategy that supports a neutral position in the organization. Generally speaking, that means a strategy rooted in productive politics, not destructive politics. Productive politics are actions and words intended to promote the organization, regardless of who personally benefits. Destructive politics, on the other hand, are actions and words intended to solely promote oneself.

To help illustrate the difference, let's say you witness a coworker make a mistake on a project. Destructive politics would look like reporting the mistake to your supervisor without the coworker's knowledge. Productive politics, on the other hand, would look like alerting the coworker to the mistake and offering insights into how it could be corrected. Figure 1.1 highlights some additional examples of destructive and productive politics.

Figure 1.1. Destructive vs. Productive Politics

Destructive	**Productive**
Gossiping and spreading rumors at someone else's expense	Limiting discussion to the business of the organization
Taking credit for someone else's work	Transparently recognizing the work of others
Focusing on the person and not the issue	Focusing on the issue and not the person
Forming alliances against colleagues with bad intent	Forming alliances with colleagues with good intent
Intentionally withholding important information	Being transparent with important information

In order to maintain a neutral political strategy focused on productive politics, you will need underlying strategies that support that position. For example, you need to understand the political landscape around you. You also need to build strong relationships with others in the organization. Finally, you need to know how to communicate in a way that is respectful of others, yet allows you to influence them and resolve conflict. All of these underlying strategies, and more, will be covered in this book.

Pulling it All Together

The business of healthcare is political, which is often not visible to the general public. Like any organization or industry, healthcare workers play political games in order to get what they want. Something I didn't realize when I started in this line of work is that the most difficult part of the job is navigating the politics of healthcare. That is not to say there aren't challenging times involved with conducting investigations or understanding the regulations. Figuring out how to effectively communicate with others though, in my opinion, requires a lot more mental energy. It is the politics, not the work of a compliance officer, that will force you to wrestle with questions like:

- "Should I raise this concern in this meeting or say something after the meeting?"
- "Who in the organization needs to know that I am working on ______?"
- "When do I need to tell others about ______?"
- "How will my decision about ______ impact my job and my department?"
- "How will my decision about ______ impact this operational department and the organization?"
- "Who is going to read what I have written?"

- "If I tell my primary audience about _____, will it get repeated to others without my knowledge?"

As we move forward in this book, we will talk through the key strategies that will help you with navigating these kinds of questions. We will start this discussion in chapter two by covering the strategy of understanding the political landscape around you.

Chapter Takeaways

- The business of healthcare is political.
- Healthcare organizations have two agendas: the business agenda and the compliance program agenda.
- Healthcare organizations are political entities in and of themselves with individuals holding formal and informal power.
- To successfully navigate the politics of healthcare, you need to develop a neutral political strategy rooted in a productive politics.
- A neutral political strategy requires skills in understanding one's political landscape, developing strong relationships with leaders, and using strong interpersonal communication skills.

Chapter Two

Understanding Your Political Landscape

The hardest thing to learn in life is
which bridge to cross and which one to burn.
—David Russell

Assume you are the new compliance officer for ABC Medical Center. You have been with the organization for two months. You receive an anonymous complaint alleging a cardiologist has snooped in another physician's medical record, potentially in violation of the Privacy Rule under the Health Insurance Portability and Accountability Act of 1996 (HIPAA).[5] This particular cardiologist is a significant referral source of patients to the hospital. Upon receiving the complaint, you identify the need to investigate. How would you go about conducting your investigation?

Aside from the obvious of conducting due diligence in investigating the facts of the matter, if it were me, I would also include understanding any background and history on the parties involved. For example, some questions I'd ponder include the following:

- Does the cardiologist or the patient/physician hold any formal power within the organization (e.g., a medical directorship or other physician leadership position)?
- Have these physicians had a history of influencing decisions within the organization?

- Has the cardiologist's business relationship with the hospital been harmonious or not so much?
- What about the relationship between the cardiologist and the patient/physician (do they get along, or do they have a strained relationship)?
- Is this cardiologist the only one on the medical staff, or are there other cardiologists on staff from the same practice or a different practice?
- Which physicians on the medical staff are partners in the practice of this cardiologist?

While these factors must not affect the conclusion of your investigation, they are important for determining the most effective way to approach your work of investigating the matter.

When it comes to navigating the politics of healthcare, your starting point is understanding the political landscape around you. This is true whether you are joining a new-to-you organization or encountering a new leader, department, or issue for the first time at an existing organization. While understanding the political landscape is the starting point, you will be actively engaged in this line of thinking throughout your career no matter where you work.

If you are new to an organization, orienting to the political landscape can easily run simultaneously with onboarding to your new role. Similarly, if you are encountering a new department, leader, or issue for the first time, understanding the political landscape should be included as part of your overall research plan. Regardless of circumstance, your approach will include one or more of the following components: (1) identifying key leaders in the organization, (2) identifying key players in your market, and (3) developing and maintaining political awareness. Let's take a look at each of these in more detail.

Identifying Key Leaders in the Organization

When it comes to starting a new job, I tend to think of those first few months as similar to walking into a social gathering for the first time. When you first walk in, you're not quite oriented to your surroundings. You don't fully realize that some of the individuals around you are people you actually know. It just feels like a room full of strangers. At some point, though, mysteriously, you do orient to your surroundings and gain a sense of who is around you. For example, you realize the two people in the corner talking are Joe and Colin, a couple of close friends of yours. On the other side of the room is Mary, your neighbor down the street. Orienting to an organization feels very similar. At first your coworkers appear to be a group of strangers, but over time you'll get to know them, their roles in the organization, and their backgrounds.

For purposes of discussion, I broadly define a "key leader" to be anyone making business decisions for the organization with whom you routinely work. A key leader could be a member of your C-suite, a medical director, or another clinical leader. It could also be a department director, manager, or supervisor. "Key leaders" will be a term you will have to define for yourself. If you are new to healthcare, Figure 2.1 includes a generic listing of key leaders common to most healthcare organizations providing patient care.

Figure 2.1. Key Leaders

- Board chair
- Board of directors
- Chief executive officer (CEO)
- Chief operating officer (COO)
- Chief financial officer (CFO)
- Chief nursing officer (CNO)
- Chief medical officer (CMO)
- General Counsel (GC)
- Department directors (clinical or administrative)
- Medical directors

If you are new to an organization, I strongly encourage you to identify your key leaders shortly after your first day on the job. If the opportunity doesn't present itself organically, then initiate a discussion with your supervisor to identify these individuals. In preparing for this discussion, it will be helpful to get ahold of an organizational chart to review. Once you have identified your key leaders, the next step is setting up a meet and greet with each one on your list.

Meet and greets have several benefits as they relate to understanding your political landscape. First, you gain an understanding of the key leader's role in the organization. Whom does this leader report to? Which departments or personnel does he or she oversee? Which departments interact with this leader's department? This information becomes invaluable when you need to leverage a leader's support to fulfill a compliance program need. For example, if the leader has staff who haven't completed mandatory training, establishing a connection with the leader can make it easier to ask for assistance in ensuring the employees complete their training.

Another benefit to these meetings is that you find out how the leader operates. You get a sense of their personality, management style, and work ethic. For example, think about the meeting itself. Were you successful in setting a time to meet, or did they repeatedly reschedule? Were they diligent to start the meeting on time, or were they late? Did they seem genuinely interested to talk to you or appear distracted?

Additionally, you can pick up any behavioral characteristics, such as communication style (e.g., a direct or indirect communicator). This can be a beneficial insight when trying to figure out how best to communicate with the leader going forward. For example, let's assume a compliance concern is identified affecting the leader's department, and this particular leader communicates directly (i.e., gets to the point). If you outline the issue succinctly, it will be received more positively than if you get bogged down in details. I say this because not being direct with direct communicators was something I struggled with early in my career when communicating with physicians.

Finally, these meetings can also be your entry point into developing political awareness. We will dive deeper into this topic later on in this chapter. For now, note that when you set up a meet and greet, the discussion can segue into a particular topic. If it does, you may start to see some of the leader's political self-interests come out. For example, maybe he or she will express a strong opinion about compliance risk involving an organizational process that hasn't been resolved.

Aside from the benefits identified above, meet and greets can also be helpful in establishing rapport with key leaders, something we'll cover in more detail in chapter five. For now, note that taking a few minutes to put a face with a name is always time well spent. It helps in creating a personal connection that you just don't get with a phone call, video call, email, text, or instant message. I have found that once I have established that personal connection with a leader, he or she tends to demonstrate an increased buy-in to the compliance program.

While much of the above discussion is in the context of being new to an organization, meet and greets are also effective when you've been with an organization for some time. Inevitably, as you are working on an investigation or other compliance matter, you will encounter a new leader or department for the first time. When you do, you can always take time to set up a meet and greet with a new-to-you leader.

Taking the time to identify the key leaders in your organization is your starting point to understanding the political landscape around you. The more you build connections with the key leaders, the more you will come to understand how they think and operate. This will become valuable insight as you move forward in the approach of your compliance work.

> ***Quick Tip: Identifying Key Leaders***
>
> **Get to *Know* Them.** Once you have identified your key leaders, find out as much as you can about them, such as their role in the organization, their professional background, and any significant positive and negative relationships with others. This can be accomplished through simple internet searches and talking with your supervisor.

Identifying Key Players in Your Market

Another element to understanding your political landscape is identifying the key players in your market. This is especially true during times when you're working on a concern relating to a business relationship with another organization. For purposes of discussion, I generically define "key players" as participants in your organization's market who shape how healthcare services are delivered in that market. More specifically, a key player could be another healthcare provider who is a business partner or competitor of your organization. For example, let's say you are the compliance officer for XYZ Orthopedics, P.C. (XYZ). A key player could be the local hospitals that XYZ is contracted with to provide orthopedic services, or even other competing physician practices. A key player could also be the insurance companies that XYZ is contracted with as a network provider. Lastly, a key player could also be various government agencies with oversight to XYZ's operations. Similar to identifying key leaders, you will have to define a "key player" for yourself based on your surroundings. Figure 2.2 includes some basic questions you can ask to help identify your key players.

Figure 2.2 Identifying Key Players

- Which organizations are business partners to your organization?
- Which organizations are competitors in your market?
- Who are the key physicians in your market?
- Who are other key healthcare professionals in your market?
- Which payers have a presence in your market, and which ones are contracted with your organization?
- Who are the legislators in your market (federal and state)?
- Which legislators control healthcare legislation?
- Who are your community leaders (e.g., city council, planning committee)?
- Which government health programs operate in your market?

Knowing the key players is a significant factor to understanding your political landscape. Knowing who these individuals are identifies external pressure points that may be motivating the decisions of your key leaders. Once you have identified the key players in your market, you need to be mindful of the relationships these individuals have with your organization. This knowledge puts you in a more informed position to find compliant and business friendly solutions for your leaders, which helps you in navigating the politics of healthcare.

Quick Tip: Identifying Key Players.

Ask Your Key Leaders About the Key Players. Consider incorporating the questions from Figure 2.2 into your meet and greet with your key leaders. This approach can reveal valuable insight or even identify additional key players you had not uncovered.

Developing and Maintaining Political Awareness

As healthcare industry workers, we all have our own sets of needs and emotions that drive our decisions and communications with others. Oftentimes the politics of healthcare sneaks in when there are differences of opinion or personality. For that reason, another element to understanding your political landscape is developing and maintaining what I like to call "political awareness." Being politically aware means you're mindful of the self-interests around you as you work on a compliance matter. Let's take a look at three main elements of political awareness: (1) Being Observant of the Relationships around You, (2) Identifying Formal and Informal Power, and (3) Identifying the Usual Suspects of Office Politics.

Being Observant of the Relationships around You

Recall my earlier analogy of starting a new job feeling like walking into a social event for the first time. When you are politically aware, it will feel like you have hit the point when you know everyone in the room. You start to notice working relationships of those around you—things like which employees are a little testy with one another. You know, maybe John and Rebecca applied for the same lab director position;

John got passed over and now reports to Rebecca. And John doesn't like it. If you asked Rebecca, I'm sure she isn't too thrilled about it either.

You may also notice which employees are a little chummy with one another. I once worked with a couple of department directors who always, and I mean always, had lunch together. They would sit next to each other during meetings, and every time there was a work event, there they were, side-by-side. Eventually, I learned they were neighbors and both had kids who went to the same school.

Whether it is a power struggle or a closely held alignment, be observant of the relationships around you. It will become valuable information for how you approach your work when it comes to things like conducting investigations. For example, if you are investigating a matter involving two people with a contentious relationship, it will factor into the credibility weight you give to their opinions about the matter or each other. Figure 2.3 includes some basic political landscape questions you can ask yourself about the relationships around you.

Figure 2.3. Basic Political Landscape Questions

- Who gets along with others?
- Who doesn't get along with others?
- Who is involved in conflict?
- Who is a part of a group, clique, or social network in the organization?
- Which staff members seem competitive?
- Which staff members seem jealous?
- Who is respected in a department or across the organization?

Identifying Formal and Informal Power

Recall back to chapter one when I mentioned that you will have individuals in your organization who hold formal and informal power. Another example of being politically aware is figuring out who holds these types of power. In terms of formal power, where do certain individuals rank in comparison to others on the organizational chart? That becomes key information when determining who to pursue for support on a compliance matter.

In the context of informal power, your focus is on who in the organization has the position or ability to influence the decisions of others. It's not always the case that it's the person with the higher rank in the organization. A lot of work in a corporate setting is based on the groupthink model. For example, a CEO may pull a committee of individuals together with the intent of having them provide their input to help the CEO shape his or her business decisions. Earlier I mentioned that a key leader's political self-interest may become apparent during an initial meet and greet. If that opportunity doesn't present itself, once you spend time in the organization, political self-interests will start to become evident. As you attend operational meetings, you'll start to pick up on who has a strong opinion about a particular issue and whom the CEO relies upon in making decisions.

Informal power isn't limited to those who influence the CEO. Across the organization, you will find that other executives, senior managers, department directors, and supervisors value the opinions of certain employees in the organization. Identifying who holds informal power becomes valuable intel during times when you need support for the compliance program's agenda. Just keep in mind that obtaining this knowledge takes months, sometimes years as you live with the organization. If you are new to healthcare, Figure 2.4 includes some questions that you can address to help identify formal and informal power in your organization.

Figure 2.4. Formal and Informal Power Questions

- Who holds formal power in a department and across the organization?
- Who has the most influence on decisions being made in a department and across the organization?
- Who has authority in a department and across the organization but doesn't act on it?
- Who is respected in a department and across the organization?
- Who holds others accountable in a department and across the organization?
- Who mentors others?

Identifying the Usual Suspects of Office Politics

No matter what organization you work for, you will have what I like to call the "Usual Suspects of Office Politics." Generally speaking, these folks like to engage in various forms of destructive politics that I mentioned in chapter one. Since our political strategy is focused on remaining neutral in the organization, you need to know how to manage your interactions with these folks. If you don't, you may unwittingly end up an accomplice to their cause. When that happens, you jeopardize your ability to effectively navigate the politics of healthcare. So, let's take a look at this cast of characters, so you know what to look out for.

The Gossiper

Starting with the most obvious, we have The Gossiper. This person seems to know *everything* about everyone and takes great pleasure in telling you about it. The Gossiper lacks discretion or a filter. Since their conduct can be destructive in an organization, it is best to identify The Gossiper, be mindful of their motives, and not enable their behavior.

Managing The Gossiper

The best way to manage your interactions with The Gossiper is to keep your conversations limited to business, thereby cutting off a potential food source for this individual.

The Toady

Call it what you will ("fawning," "brown-nosing," "bootlicking"), The Toady likes to flatter people with compliments, especially those with a superior position in the organization. The problem with The Toady is that the comments aren't genuine. They're purely for personal gain. When it comes to The Toady, the good news is that the disingenuous behavior is easy to detect and obvious to everyone. Everyone except The Toady, of course.

Managing The Toady

The best way to manage your interactions with The Toady is to be aware of their ulterior motive and identify *the why* behind the flattery. What advantage is this person trying to gain? Be cautious about how much credibility to give them. For the most part, let The Toady do their toady thing. Most healthcare leaders know when someone is being fake.

The Saboteur

Next, we have The Saboteur. Arguably on the other end of the spectrum from The Toady, this person's objective is not to compliment for personal gain, but rather disrupt for personal gain. This individual thrives off being critical of others, especially in public settings, like a meeting or conference call. The Saboteur can also have passive-aggressive tendencies such as forwarding your email onto others without your knowledge, or replying to your email, along with a laundry list of others, including your supervisor. If throwing people under the bus were an Olympic sport, this person would be a gold medalist—every time.

Managing The Saboteur

The best way to manage The Saboteur is to be cautious when communicating with this individual. And think at least two steps ahead. For example, if you send The Saboteur an email, expect that it will get forwarded to others. Thinking ahead will ensure your communication is professional and defendable. Also, keep your focus on the matter being addressed, and not the individual. If you allow The Saboteur to see your frustration, he or she will seize the moment to use it against you.

The Debater

The Debater loves nothing more in life than playing devil's advocate. They typically are argumentative and quick on their feet. They're also not afraid to twist facts to fit their agenda. The Debater is also one you need to be cautious with in your communications. Dialogue in a meeting that is productive to the group's objective is healthy and should be encouraged. Where you can get into trouble is when debate becomes about the other person and not the group's objective. The Debater loves to provoke others, so be cautious not to take the bait. Make sure the points you are making are about the group's objective, not The Debater.

Managing The Debater

The best way to manage The Debater is to give them space; allow them to be heard. That said, to avoid a conversation spiraling into a never-ending argument, acknowledge and validate their point. Then maintain your focus on accomplishing the goal of the discussion.

The Credit Poacher

One of my personal favorites is The Credit Poacher. Another disingenuous type, this individual will do whatever it takes to get ahead in the organization, even if it means stealing some ideas and the work of others and passing it off as his or her own.

Managing The Credit Poacher

The best way to manage The Credit Poacher is to be aware of their presence and share your ideas and work product publicly whenever possible. You can also frequently update your supervisor so he or she knows who should be getting credit for the work. If you feel there is a legitimate need to call out The Credit Poacher, the best way to do so is to discuss the matter confidentially with the appropriate leader instead of in a public setting.

The Delegator

Next up is The Delegator. To be clear, the person I'm referring to here is not your supervisor, who of course is empowered to delegate tasks to you. Instead, this particular individual delegates tasks they are not in a position to delegate. Sometimes you'll see this surface when you volunteer a thought or idea, but rather than your supervisor or a project leader delegating a task to you, someone else on the team does. The Delegator tends to believe the act of delegation is a demonstration of power. The only problem is The Delegator doesn't actually have the power.

Managing The Delegator

The best way to manage The Delegator is to make sure the task being delegated is within the scope of your role in the organization. If it is, then the request is legitimate and you need to be a business partner by following up on the task. If it is not, then you need to communicate what tasks fall within your role. Regardless of circumstance, if you have a concern about others inappropriately delegating, it is best to confidentially communicate those concerns to the appropriate leader to address with the employee.

The Advisor

Saving the best for last, we come to The Advisor. Now, unlike all the other characters mentioned above, The Advisor tends be engaged in productive politics. This particular individual is one to whom other healthcare leaders in your organization turn for assistance. They tend to maintain a lot of influence in the organization and have an awareness of what is going on. For that reason, The Advisor can be an asset to you and not a liability.

Managing The Advisor

The best way to manage your interactions with The Advisor is to align with this individual. These folks tend to hold informal power in the organization, which can help you in advancing the compliance program's agenda when you need leverage or support.

Whether you are involved in a conference call, a meeting, a hallway discussion—or my personal favorite, the meeting after the meeting—pay attention to your surroundings. Pay attention to what's being said, how it is being said, and who is saying it. These are continual opportunities to observe a wealth of information orienting you to the political landscape around you.

Bonus material: For tips on how to gather intel to become more politically aware in your organization, visit my Intel Tips Sheet at: http://www.bluebirdhealthlaw.com/book-bonuses.

Quick Tip: Developing and Maintaining Political Awareness

Factor in Your Landscape. Include the topic of political landscape as part of anything you are working on. Whether you are consulting on a proposed business deal, delivering training, or conducting an investigation, knowing the personality types, the relationships, and the history helps you in determining how best to proceed.

Pulling it All Together

Having a sense of the political landscape around you is a key strategy for navigating the politics of healthcare. This information will be invaluable to you for several reasons. First, you will be a more informed compliance officer. This improves your ability to find solutions that accommodate your organization's business and compliance program agenda. Second, you will better understand *the why* behind the decisions made in the organization. Finally, you will be in a better position to predict the political objections from your leaders and proactively address them. Now that we have taken a look at understanding the political landscape around you, in chapters three and four, we will discuss another key strategy—thinking like a healthcare leader.

Chapter Takeaways

- A key strategy for navigating the politics of healthcare is understanding the political landscape around you.
- Understanding your political landscape includes (1) identifying key leaders, (2) identifying key players, and (3) developing and maintaining political awareness.
- Obtaining this information better positions you to predict politics-based objections from your leaders and proactively address them.
- Understanding the political landscape around you supports a neutral political strategy in the organization.

Chapter Three

Thinking Like a Healthcare Leader—Part One

You can only understand people if you feel them in yourself.
—John Steinbeck

Assume for a moment you're not a compliance officer. You're the chief executive officer (CEO) of ABC Hospital, and you're looking to expand the hospital's service line. During a recent strategic planning meeting, your chief operating officer (COO) pitches an idea: "What if we partnered with a XYZ Cardiology, P.C. (XYZ) to open a new clinic focused on vascular services?" The idea piques your interest. With the assistance of legal counsel, you move forward. You negotiate and sign compliant agreements with XYZ and set a go-live date.

During your most recent meeting with the cardiologists, there was discussion about a need to market this new venture and who would pay for it. The physicians are asking the hospital to bear the costs of marketing because the new clinic is going to be located on the hospital's campus. You email your compliance officer to ask if the hospital can pay for these expenses since the physicians will be benefiting from the marketing. Your compliance officer responds by saying no. She doesn't offer an explanation. She doesn't ask any questions about the venture or the marketing campaign. She doesn't even offer an alternative option. If you were this CEO, would you feel supported?

A consistent theme in all of the strategies we will cover in this book is being mindful of your audience. This is particularly important when it comes to healthcare leaders. That means at times, you need to be thinking like a healthcare leader—not a compliance officer. That means listening to what they're telling you, and approaching your work with consideration of their viewpoint, not yours. If you are a leader, what obstacles or challenges do you face? What motivates you in the performance of your role? What political pressures do you face? These are just some of the questions you need to be thinking about when communicating with your healthcare leaders about compliance matters.

Having an awareness for how your leaders think will help you in navigating the politics of healthcare. You will understand why certain decisions are made, recognize why you are getting pushback, and have the ability to anticipate future decisions. In order to think like a healthcare leader, we need to climb into their minds. Since there are a number of healthcare leaders to cover, we'll start the discussion in this chapter, and then finish it up in chapter four.

Identifying a Healthcare Leader's Point-of-View

A significant step toward thinking like a healthcare leader is identifying their point of view (POV). While POV is specific to a leader's role, personality, and the issue being addressed, there are some POVs that apply to most healthcare leaders. For example, consider the topic of change—I mean from an evolutionary standpoint, not a monetary one. Healthcare at a very basic level is a service industry. Considering that a leader's role and objectives are to move the organization forward, leaders must continually embrace change in order to succeed. As a consequence, implementing newer, faster, or better ways to deliver healthcare will always be a factor in the mind of your healthcare leaders. As the compliance officer, you have to accept that leaders will always be pushing for change. Change is not a bad thing, though. It means new questions to wrestle with, and that translates into growth opportunities and job security for you.

Another universally held POV is determining what is in the best interest of the patient. With any business decision a healthcare leader makes, that question floats across the brain. Overall, this POV is focused on what is safe and of high quality yet practical and efficient. A final example of a universal POV among healthcare leaders is determining what is in the best interest of the organization. Here, this POV is focused on ensuring the organization is moving forward within the market while protecting it from financial, legal, and reputational risk.

Now that we have explored some universally held leadership POVs, let's walk through a list of typical leaders in a hospital or other patient care related organization. We will look at their roles and responsibilities, what shapes their POV, how they think, and how to approach your work from the viewpoint of the leader.

Governing Board

The governing board is the highest authority within a healthcare organization. The governing board may be referred to as the board of directors, board of managers, or board of trustees, depending upon how the organization is set up from a legal standpoint. The governing body is responsible for developing and reviewing the organization's overall mission and strategy. For purposes of discussion, I will refer to the governing body simply as the "board" and the individuals as "board members."

For larger organizations, the board members typically run other organizations or otherwise have full-time positions elsewhere. For smaller organizations, such as a large physician practice, the board will consist of shareholder physicians in the practice. A board typically meets periodically, often monthly or quarterly. While this schedule is reasonable, considering the board members' other responsibilities, there can be continuity challenges due to gaps in time between meetings. Additionally, because the board is not involved in the organization's day-to-day operations, board members typically have limited knowledge or understanding of particular issues that arise. Depending upon the size of the board, some of their work may be carried out through various committees.

Some examples include a finance committee, operations committee, and compliance committee. The committees meet as needed in between the meetings of the full board.

When it comes to the staff within the organization, the board is primarily focused on the one employee who reports to them: the CEO. That is not to say that other senior leaders aren't important. Rather, it boils down to the fact the board doesn't supervise those leaders; the CEO does. The board hires the CEO, sets his or her goals and objectives, and evaluates his or her performance. Depending upon the organization's corporate culture, a delicate balance of roles can exist between the board and the CEO. In some corporate cultures, the board may take an active role in the management of the organization. For example, you may see this in smaller organizations, such as a large physician practice. In larger organizations, like a health system, the board will take a more passive role, allowing the CEO to exercise autonomy. While healthcare organizations differ, some basic responsibilities the board has include the following:

- **Setting and following strategic direction.** The board will have final authority to determine the long-term strategic business direction of the organization.
- **Management oversight.** The board has responsibility for monitoring and evaluating the performance of the CEO.
- **Financial oversight.** The board has final authority with respect to decisions affecting the organization's finances.

- **Quality of care oversight.** If the organization provides patient care, the board will be responsible for ensuring that certain quality of care benchmarks are being met.
- **Compliance Program Oversight.** If the organization has a compliance program in place, the board will have oversight for the compliance program and review of the program's function and activities.

The size of a board will also vary depending upon the size of the organization and legal structure. Regardless of size, a consistent trait of all boards is that they will have an appointed leader (e.g., a board chairperson), who will administratively oversee the operations of the board . These are typically elected positions with set terms.

A Word about Fiduciary Duties

When it comes to board members themselves, there are certain fiduciary duties the individuals must maintain as part of their oversight role for the organization. These fiduciary duties include (1) duty of care, (2) duty of loyalty, and (3) duty of obedience.

The duty of care provides the board members must act in good faith, with the same level of care a prudent person would show in the same circumstances. This means the board members must make decisions that are financially, legally, and ethically sound. Board members must be present, informed, and engaged to make the best decisions for the organization by using independent judgment and staying current on operational developments.

The duty of loyalty provides that board members must act in the best interests of the organization and never in their own interests. This means board members must put the interests of the organization before their own interests. For example, if the organization is in need of contracted services, and the spouse of board member Anstine provides those services, then board member Anstine must be removed from a decision of whether or not to use the spouse's company. As part of this duty, the organization must have a conflict of interest policy, and the board members must disclose any real or perceived conflicts of interest.

The duty of obedience provides that board members must ensure that their decisions are in line with the law—more specifically, ensuring that the organization is following all laws and regulations applicable to its line of business.

Thinking Like a Board Member

When it comes to a board member's POV, they are motivated by what is in the best interest of the organization. This viewpoint takes into account strategic, financial, legal, and reputational concerns. From a strategic perspective, they ensure that the organization is meeting the goals and objectives set by the board. From a financial perspective, they must ensure that the board members are acting as good stewards of the organization's financial resources and that the organization is meeting certain financial goals. From a legal perspective, board members seek to ensure the organization and the individuals operating it are not conducting themselves in a manner that creates liability. Finally, from a reputational standpoint, they must ensure that the organization is acting as a good business partner within the community. Figure 3.1 includes a sample of some of the political pressures board members face that shape their POV.

Figure 3.1. Board Member Political Pressures

- Expectation from shareholders to reduce financial, legal, and reputational risk
- Expectation from themselves to do what is in the best interest of the organization
- Expectation from themselves to avoiding personal liability
- Expectation from shareholders to fulfill their fiduciary duties
- Expectation from the board chair to carry out any required committee work reportable to the full board
- The government and the compliance officer expecting the Board to ensure the organization remains compliant with all laws and regulations

Positioning Compliance for a Board Member's POV

When it comes to approaching your work as a compliance officer, be mindful of who this audience is in the organization. That means understanding their roles and responsibilities as the governing board as well as taking into account their political pressures. Since the board has oversight for the compliance program, your interests should be aligned. Relatedly, as the organization's governing body, the board has the responsibility for setting the organization's corporate culture of compliance. That means leading by example when it comes to ethical decision making.

Keep in mind these individuals likely do not have healthcare regulatory experience. They will not be as knowledgeable about compliance programs and the rules and regulations as you are. For that reason, you may need to take a step back and explain terminology you might not otherwise have to think about. It's kind of like trying to explain to a four-year-old what the word "anyway" means. There are some words we get so close to because we use them all the time that we never even think about actually defining them. The point here is if you assume they know nothing, it will help ensure that your communication logically flows from one point to the next. It also cuts down on the time you have to spend responding to questions.

> ***Quick Tip: Governing Board***
>
> **Build strong relationships with your board.** Since the board has the ultimate authority for your compliance program, they can serve as an ally to help provide support, such as conducting an investigation of a member of senior management or influencing their behavior, both of which would be considered political (or sensitive).

Chief Executive Officer (CEO)

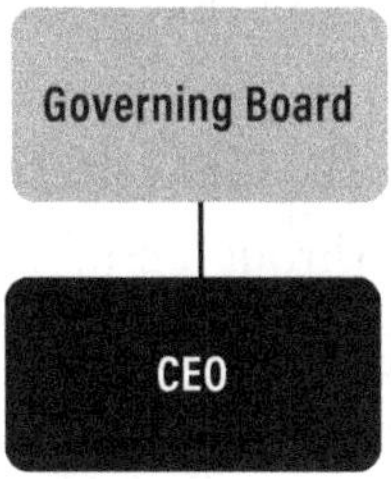

As the highest-level healthcare administrator, the CEO has the overall responsibility for the organization's day-to-day operations and fulfilling its strategic vision. CEO positions are often filled by individuals possessing business backgrounds; however, there has been an increasing trend of CEOs possessing a clinical background too (e.g., an MD or RN). While the exact CEO responsibilities will vary by organization, they likely will include the following:

- **Organizational vision.** The CEO must have a vision for the organization's future, such as an identified market presence or access to high-quality healthcare.

- **Strategic planning.** The CEO must have an identified roadmap of future goals and objectives for achieving the organizational vision.
- **Maintaining financial stability.** The CEO needs to ensure the organization maintains financial health and stability. If the organization is a tax-exempt organization, there are additional responsibilities for ensuring it is meeting its charitable mission.
- **Recruitment.** The CEO must ensure the organization has the physicians and other clinical staff to meet the needs of providing services to the community.
- **Patient safety.** The CEO must ensure patients are cared for safely through established safety measures.
- **Promoting high-quality healthcare.** The CEO must be committed to improving the quality of healthcare provided to the organization's patients.
- **Patient satisfaction.** The CEO must ensure the organization is meeting established patient satisfaction benchmarks.
- **Organizational compliance.** The CEO must ensure the organization is maintaining compliance with all federal, state, and local laws and regulations, and maintaining a healthy culture of compliance.

In order to carry out these responsibilities, the CEO needs to fulfill several different roles. First and foremost, the CEO is a business leader. He or she must balance the management of operations against the organization's finances to ensure it is effectively utilizing resources. CEOs of organizations providing patient care must additionally manage the added pressure of competition from other market participants.

The CEO must also fill the role of politician. Hospital CEOs continually have to manage communications and relationships. Since CEOs are responsible for overseeing a number of different operations, akin to those of a small town, the CEO *is* the face of this community, much like a mayor is for a city. That requires being adept at knowing what information needs to be shared with constituents and when it needs to be shared. Externally, the CEO has to manage relationships with several parties, such as business partners (e.g., physicians), business competitors, government regulators, community leaders, patients (and their families), and the media. Given the demands in managing all these relationships, they must be skilled in communication and conflict resolution. When it comes to a day in the life of a CEO, their schedules are typically packed from early morning meetings to business dinners lasting well into the evening.

Thinking Like a CEO

A CEO's POV is going to be shaped by fulfilling the organization's identified objectives that support the overall strategic plan approved by the board. With that said, many of the decisions a CEO has to make can be traced to one of three self-interests. First, what is in the best interest of the patient? That is true whether the matter is starting a new service line, resolving a complaint, or terminating a physician from the medical staff. Second, what is in the best interest of the organization? Whether it's a business decision of the CEO or any of his or her direct reports, CEOs are motivated by the ones that result in the least amount of legal, financial, or reputational risk. Finally, the CEOs are motivated by acting in the best interests of their own careers. I'm not saying that to be judgmental, but rather, as a matter of fact. We're all motivated to act in the best interest of our careers. As part of the organization's strategic plan and objectives, the board will be evaluating the CEO on how he or she is performing based on criteria set by the board. Figure 3.2 includes a sample of typical political pressures CEOs face that shape their POV.

Figure 3.2. CEO Political Pressures

- The community expecting the CEO to deliver high-quality, low cost patient care services
- The board expecting the CEO to do more with fewer resources
- The department leaders expecting the CEO to provide more resources
- The physicians expecting the CEO to increase their compensation and have more control over clinical decisions
- The employees expecting the CEO to be a great leader (inspiring and visionary)
- The community leaders expecting the CEO to be an active participant who is contributing to the community
- The board expecting the CEO to be competitive in the market
- The government and the compliance officer expecting the CEO to ensure the organization remains compliant with all laws and regulations

Positioning Compliance for a CEO's POV

When it comes to your work as a compliance officer, you should be thinking about it from the CEO's perspective. If you were in his or her shoes, what information would you want to know? For example, let's say you identified a potential breach of one thousand patient records. As the CEO you're going to want to know the details of what happened and how this issue was discovered. You also want to know the risk involved with a breach (e.g., financial and reputational). Finally, you want to know what steps the compliance officer is taking to correct the issue and prevent a future occurrence.

Keep in mind that depending upon the nature of the issue, the CEO may be duty-bound to report the matter to the board, so consider his or her perspective in carrying out that responsibility. As a general rule, the level of detailed information you need to provide the CEO should match the level of risk involved. For example, if you're addressing a six-figure overpayment to Medicaid, a high level of detail is needed; if it's a small refund involving a few claims, an overview or summary will do.

You also should be thinking about when to notify the CEO about what you're working on. In this context, the urgency and frequency of communication should also match the level of risk. For example, in the case of a potential breach involving one thousand patients and the obligations to notify the patients, media, and the Office for Civil Rights (OCR),[6] you're going to want to notify the CEO as soon as possible. On the other hand, if it's an investigation of an inadvertent billing error to Medicare involving a few claims, you can wait until you have all the facts and the investigation is complete. In other words, the size and scale of the matter and the associated risk will determine when you need to notify the CEO about what you are working on.

Quick Tip: CEO

Build a strong relationship with your CEO. As the highest executive and face of the organization, he or she can help you in promoting compliance to employees and contractors. He or she can also help you in overcoming resistance from others in the organization.

Chief Operating Officer (COO)

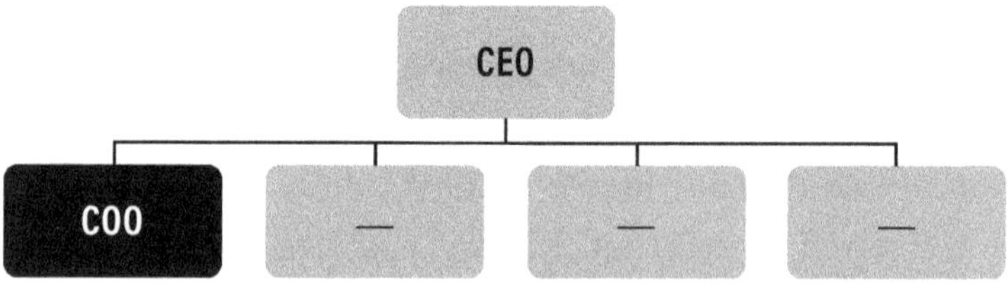

If you work for a larger organization, you may have a COO in addition to a CEO to help support the oversight and management of the operations of the organization. The COO's role is to oversee the daily operations of the organization and serve as a second in command to the CEO. It is for this reason you'll find some CEOs who were formerly COOs.

I tend to think of CEOs and COOs as similar in roles to that of the president and vice president of the United States. Relatedly, the success of an organization operationally depends upon a well-functioning relationship between these two individuals. In instances where an organization has both a COO and CEO, the CEO will retain global oversight for the organization's operations, such as mission, vision, and strategic plan. The COO will then have oversight responsibilities for the day-to-day operations that support the organization's mission, vision, and strategic plan. In a nutshell, the CEO will be responsible for what areas the organization is focused on, while the COO is responsible for *how* the organization will carry out the identified areas of focus. For this reason, COOs must have a detailed understanding of the processes and technical aspects of how the organization carries out its work. A COO's responsibilities typically include the following:

- **Operational oversight.** The COO serves as the primary administrative contact for employees and contractors (clinical or administrative).
- **Corporate culture.** The COO also is put in a position to help shape the corporate culture as it relates to the day-to-day activities of the organization.
- **Operationalizing the strategic plan.** The COO is responsible for ensuring that the operational activities support the strategic plan.
- **Organizational finances.** The COO is responsible for ensuring the organization is meeting its budget and pursuing new service lines to generate revenue.
- **Physician contracting/relations.** The COO serves as the point of contact for physician recruitment, contract negotiations, building and maintaining strong relationships, and resolving service delivery or compensation disputes.

- **Patient satisfaction/quality.** A COO may also have oversight for ensuring the organization is meeting certain quality and patient safety standards.
- **Organizational compliance.** The COO must ensure the organization is maintaining compliance with all federal, state, and local laws and regulations as well as supporting a healthy culture of compliance.

Thinking Like a COO

A COO's POV is going to be shaped by ensuring the organization's operations are meeting the objectives that support the overall strategic plan. To think like a COO means to think like a person overseeing operational logistics. This means a mindset that is focused on the big-picture impact to the organization, and the small-picture focus on details and technical processes. COOs tend to function like salespeople who are driven to find ways to generate revenue. They are also problem solvers, driven by the mental challenge of thinking creatively to find solutions to problems.

Many of the decisions of a COO can be traced to the following self-interests. First, similar to the CEO, what is in the best interest of the organization? What business relationships need to be maintained, and how can the organization ensure it remains competitive in the market? Second, how can the organization meet the operational objectives that support the overall strategic plan? Usually, the COO's performance goals are tied to hitting certain financial benchmarks such as revenue generated and budgets met. Finally, what is in the best interest of the patient? Here, the COO's performance goals are also tied to improving patient satisfaction scores and improving patient outcomes. Figure 3.3 includes a sample of typical political pressures COOs often face that shape their POV.

Figure 3.3. COO Political Pressures

- The CEO and board expecting the COO to ensure the organization is competitive in the market
- The CEO expecting the COO to do more with less
- Department leaders expecting the COO to provide more resources
- The CEO expecting the COO to maintain staff morale
- The CFO expecting the COO to hold down expenses and meet budgets
- The CEO/board expecting the COO to meet business and professional goals
- The government and the compliance officer expecting the COO to ensure the organization remains compliant with all laws and regulations

Positioning Compliance for a COO's POV

When it comes to your work as a compliance officer, be thinking about it from the COO's perspective. If you were the COO, what information would you want to know about a particular matter? The COO's perspective will largely mirror the CEO's, but the COO is going to be more connected to the operational processes of the organization. For that reason, a COO's questions are likely to be more focused on the operational logistics involved with the compliance matter at issue.

Quick Tip: COO

Build a strong relationship with your COO. As a "right hand" to the CEO, the COO can provide support when the CEO is not available. The COO also can provide a greater level of detail on the operations of the organization than the CEO.

Chief Financial Officer (CFO)

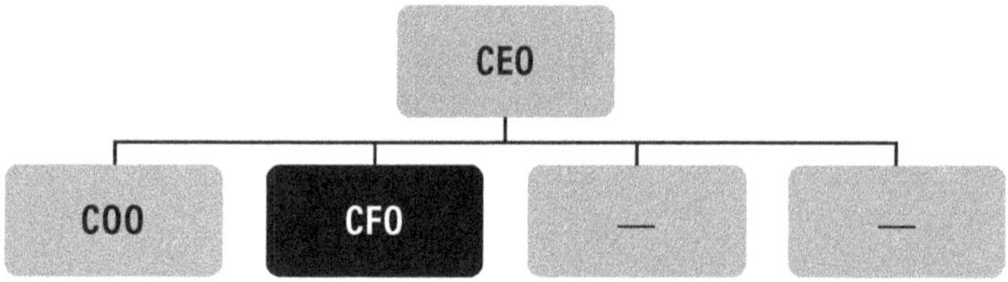

As the highest ranking financial official in the organization, the CFO has the overall responsibility of managing the organization's finances. A CFO oversees the organization's financial plans, including budgeting, taxation, and developing strategies for boosting revenue. The CFO also ensures that internal controls are in place to manage the organization's finances in a cost-effective manner. From a staffing perspective, the CFO is responsible for managing the organization's financial and accounting department personnel. The CFO also serves as spokesperson to the CEO and board related to the organization's finances. Some specific CFO responsibilities include the following:

- **Financial forecasting and budgeting.** CFOs develop and administer operating and capital expenditure budgets as well as manage income and expenses.

- **Revenue management.** CFOs oversee the organization's revenue, including strategies for increasing cash flow, billing and claims management, and investment.
- **Financial analysis and performance reporting.** CFOs routinely report out on the financial performance of the organization, including any strengths and weaknesses.
- **Contract negotiation.** CFOs help negotiate payment for vendor contracts and reimbursement from contracted payers.
- **Funding source obligations.** CFOs oversee financial obligations to funding sources (e.g., banks, commercial lenders, tax-exempt issued bonds, donors).
- **Tax filings and financial reporting.** Whether for profit or not, CFOs ensure the organization is compliant with all applicable tax filings and other reporting obligations.
- **Organizational compliance.** The CFO must ensure the organization is maintaining compliance with all federal, state, and local laws and regulations as well as supporting a healthy culture of compliance.

Thinking Like a CFO

A CFO's POV will be focused on the organization's overall financial health. Thinking like a CFO means that you are factoring in financial impact to the organization for any business decision you make. If you're discussing a compliance matter with a CFO, here are some examples of the types of questions he or she may be thinking of:

- How will this business decision impact the organization's budget?
- What steps can be taken to mitigate financial risk?
- How does this business decision impact the organization's contracts with payers?
- If the organization is tax exempt, does this impact the organization's IRS 990 filing?

Figure 3.3 includes a sample of typical political pressures CFOs face that shape their POV.

Figure 3.3. CFO Political Pressures

- The CEO/board expecting CFO to develop and administer a budget that allows the organization to drive a competitive strategy
- The CEO/board expecting the CFO to control costs and generate revenue
- Department leaders expecting the CFO to ensure the organization is keeping up with the space, equipment, staffing, and technology of its competitors
- The CEO/board expecting the CFO to meet identified financial performance goals
- The CEO expecting the CFO to negotiate favorable reimbursement rates with payers
- The government and the compliance officer expecting the CFO to ensure the organization remains compliant with all laws and regulations

Positioning Compliance for a CFO's POV

When it comes to your work as a compliance officer, be thinking about it from the CFO's perspective. If you were the CFO and listening to me, the compliance officer, what information would you want to know? For example, if you're conducting an investigation involving an identified billing error, the CFO is going to be asking questions about the financial component of the investigation. More specifically, how many patient accounts are involved? What payers need to be refunded? Does this billing error impact any cost-sharing amounts paid by the patient that also need to be refunded? Does this matter create a cost-reporting error that also needs to be corrected? And of course, similar to the CEO, the CFO is going to want to know what circumstances led to the error and what steps are being taken to correct it going forward.

Quick Tip: CFO

Build a strong relationship with your CFO. As an individual with oversight of the financial operations of the organization, the CFO can enlist support from his or her staff to assist with investigations or audits (e.g., generate claims reports, accounts receivable or accounts payable information, payer data).

Pulling it All Together

Knowing how to think like the healthcare leaders that we covered in this chapter is important to navigating the politics of healthcare. It positions you to be able to anticipate certain questions they may be asking you, or concerns they are raising about a compliance matter. In this chapter we took a look at the governing board, as well as some of the key leadership positions in a hospital or other patient care related organization. In the next chapter we will continue this discussion by looking at legal counsel as well as some of the other key leadership roles on the administrative and clinical side of the organization.

Chapter Takeaways

- All healthcare leaders have points of view, which shape their individual self-interests.
- Knowing how to think like a healthcare leader means you understand the aspects of the leaders' roles in the organization that shape their POV.
- Thinking like a healthcare leader allows you to identify their self-interest and relate to your audience, which improves your ability to obtain buy-in to the compliance program.
- When you think like a healthcare leader, you put yourself in a better position to tailor a solution fit for the organization's business and compliance program agenda.

Chapter Four

Thinking Like a Healthcare Leader—Part Two

Nobody cares how much you know
until they know how much you care.
—Theodore Roosevelt

In this chapter we're going to continue our discussion that is focused on some of the key leadership positions in a hospital setting. More specifically, we will look at the following roles:

- Chief Nursing Officer
- Legal Counsel
- Chief Medical Officer
- Department Leaders (administrative or clinical).

Similar to our discussion in the last chapter, we will look at each leader's roles and responsibilities, how to think like the leader, identifying the leader's political pressures, and how to position compliance to appeal to that leader's POV.

Chief Nursing Officer (CNO)

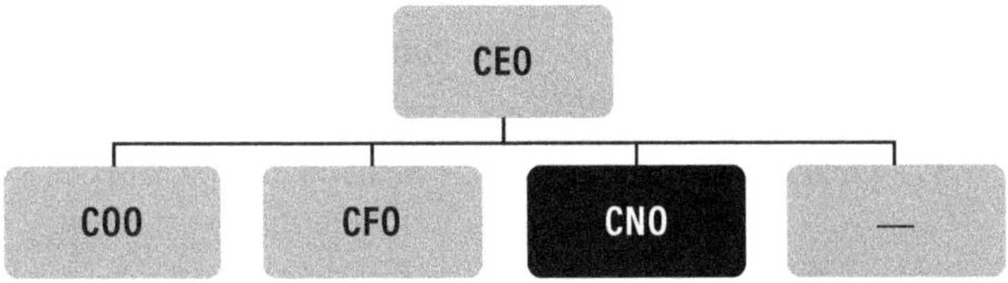

The CNO is the highest-ranking nursing leader in the organization. Overall, the CNO's role is to ensure that patient care and clinical quality standards are maintained. In fulfilling this duty, CNOs have the responsibility of overseeing the daily operations of nursing staff, which may also include other clinical staff (e.g., lab techs). CNOs tend to have significant knowledge of the organization's clinical processes and procedures as well as local, state, and federal regulations impacting clinical care services.

Similar to other senior management positions, CNOs are often excellent communicators, having spent years developing their leadership and business skills. CNOs are often highly skilled in critical thinking and strategic planning. They also have the ability to adapt quickly to unexpected changes as their clinical staff are required to do on the floor every day. While the specific duties of a CNO will vary, they often include the following:

- **Clinical operations oversight.** Overseeing the daily clinical operations of the organization, including planning, organizing, coordinating, and directing clinical care services.
- **Nursing leadership.** Serving as a nursing spokesperson to the board, other members of senior management, and the employees.
- **Physician and provider liaison.** Serving as a communication link between clinical staff and physicians or other healthcare providers.
- **Patient safety oversight.** Ensuring any patient-safety-related issues are resolved with specific steps outlined to prevent future occurrences.

- **Clinical performance.** Ensuring the organization is meeting identified clinical metrics tied to quality, reimbursement, and patient satisfaction.
- **Financial performance.** The CNO ensures clinical departments are meeting operational budgets.
- **Clinical policies and procedures.** Overseeing clinical policies and procedures to ensure they are developed, implemented, and current as well as ensuring staff are trained on them.
- **Organizational compliance.** The CNO must ensure the organization is maintaining compliance with all federal, state, and local laws and regulations as well as supporting a healthy culture of compliance.

Thinking Like a CNO

A CNO's POV is going to be shaped by three primary self-interests. First, what is the best interest of the patient? If a negative outcome occurs involving a patient, the CNO may be involved to oversee the matter. Relatedly, a CNO will be thinking about how best to provide leadership to ensure the issue is resolved and that steps are taken to prevent future occurrences. Second, what is in the best interest of the organization? Here, the CNO's focus is going to be ensuring the organization is competitive in the market and meeting certain clinical standards. For example, CNOs may implement new nursing strategies or revise existing ones to ensure patients receive high-quality, safe, and efficient care. Finally, what is in the best interest of the clinical staff? Here, the CNO's focus is going to be ensuring effective communication and processes exist to support clinical staff in making decisions that impact patient care. Figure 4.4 includes a sample of typical political pressures CNOs face that shape their POV.

Figure 4.4. CNO Political Pressures

- The CEO/board and community expecting the CNO to deliver high-quality care to patients
- The CEO/board and community expecting the CNO to keep patients safe and resolve identified clinical risk concerns involving patient care
- The CEO/CFO/board expecting the CNO to meet quality standards tied to reimbursement
- The CEO/board expecting the CNO to successfully pass organizational surveys and inspections tied to quality of care and patient safety
- The CFO expecting the CNO to meet operational budget goals and do more with less
- Department leaders expecting the CNO to keep up with the clinical staffing, equipment, and technology resources of the organization's competitors
- The physicians expecting the CNO is to resolve workflow concerns involving physicians and clinical staff members
- The government and the compliance officer expecting the CNO to ensure the organization remains compliant with all laws and regulations

Positioning Compliance for a CNO's POV

When it comes to your work as a compliance officer, be thinking about it from the CNO's perspective, which means there are two areas of focus. First, how does your work impact patients? Second, how does it impact clinical staff? For example, assume you were communicating with the CNO about a new regulatory change affecting operations. What impact will this change have on the communication between staff who are serving the patients? Will new policies and procedures, forms, or checklists need to be developed? Who will be responsible for implementing them? Who needs to be trained on the new changes, and who is responsible for conducting the training? These are just examples of some of the questions you need to anticipate a CNO may ask you as you work together on a compliance matter.

Quick Tip: CNO

Build a strong relationship with your CNO. As an individual with clinical oversight for the organization, he or she is going to be deeply knowledgeable about clinical processes and procedures. For that reason, CNOs can provide you valuable insight into clinical operations and help enlist clinical staff to support your compliance program activities.

Chief Medical Officer (CMO)

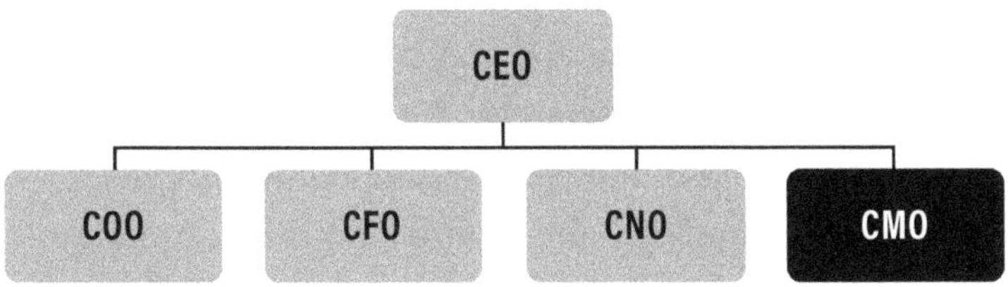

A CMO has the overall responsibility for ensuring that safe, effective, and high-quality care is delivered to patients by physicians on the medical staff. CMOs are typically physicians who have made a shift from clinical practice to an administrative role, either on a part-time or full-time basis. The CMO is a liaison role between the hospital and various internal and external parties. These parties may include other members of senior management, the board, and community business partners, as well as patients and their families. The CMO represents the hospital but also serves as a spokesperson for the employed or contracted physicians on the medical staff. While the specific duties of a CMO will vary, they typically involve the following:

- **Physician services operational oversight.** Overseeing all clinical operations involving physicians on the medical staff.
- **Established clinical performance goals.** Defining and monitoring clinical performance to ensure goals are met by the medical staff.
- **Quality improvement.** Overseeing any quality improvement activities involving physicians on the medical staff.
- **Policies and procedures.** Assisting with policy and procedure development specific to the medical staff (e.g., organizational policies, medical staff bylaws, medical staff rules and regulations).
- **Accreditation oversight.** Assisting departments or organizations in obtaining and maintaining accreditation (e.g., The Joint Commission, American College of Radiology).
- **Financial oversight.** Assisting the organization in developing cost-containment strategies that involve the

medical staff, in addition to ensuring that quality-based metrics tied to reimbursement are met.

- **Strategic planning.** Participating in long-range planning of the organization, including decisions related to equipment, budgeting, and physician staffing.
- **Education.** Facilitating educational offerings to physicians on the medical staff or offerings to the community.
- **Resolving identified issues.** Assisting with physician-to-physician communication as well as communication with patients and their families to resolve clinical care concerns.
- **Organizational compliance.** The CMO must ensure the organization is maintaining compliance with all federal, state, and local laws and regulations as well as supporting a healthy culture of compliance.

In order to carry out these responsibilities, physician leaders need to be excellent communicators, adept at conflict resolution, and possess the technical skills to step in and review either a physician's performance or a department's clinical processes.

Thinking Like a CMO

The POV of a CMO is going to be shaped by three primary interests. First, what is in the best interest of the patient? As a medically trained physician, the CMO is predisposed to be thinking about all operational decisions that need to be made from the perspective of the patient. Second, what is in the best interest of the organization? Here, the CMO's focus is ensuring the physicians on the medical staff are following the organization's policies and procedures as well as all applicable regulatory requirements. Additionally, the CMO will be motivated by fulfilling the organization's strategic plan by being competitive in the market and providing high-quality care. Finally, what is in the best interest of the physicians? Given the CMO's role, all physicians on the medical staff, regardless of specialty, are going to be the CMO's constituency. The CMO serves as a voice for them as he or she resolves identified issues with the hospital or any external parties (e.g., patient, government agency). Figure 4.5 includes a sample of typical political pressures CMOs face that shape their POV.

Figure 4.5. CMO Political Pressures

- The CEO/board and community expecting the CMO to deliver high-quality care to patients
- The physicians on the medical staff expecting the CMO to fight for what they think is the right
- The CEO/board expecting the CMO to keep the physicians "in line" with policies, directives, and business goals of the organization
- The CEO/board expecting the CMO to resolve any clinical performance or behavior-related concerns involving physicians on the medical staff
- The CFO expecting the CMO to meet operational budget goals and do more with less
- The physicians expecting the CMO to keep up with the clinical staffing, equipment, and technology resources of the organization's competitors
- The physicians expecting the CMO to resolve workflow concerns involving physicians and clinical staff members
- The government and the compliance officer expecting the CMO to ensure the organization remains compliant with all laws and regulations

Positioning Compliance for a CMO's POV

When it comes to your work as a compliance officer, be thinking about it from the CMO's perspective—which is to say, like a physician. Physicians are a unique audience when it comes to communication. We will dive into how to communicate diplomatically with physicians in chapter five. For now, just note that CMOs are physicians, so what you are telling the CMO is going to be interpreted from the vantage point of a physician and how patients are going to be impacted. Any time you have a need to speak with a physician about a compliance matter, it is best to have a CMO, or another appropriate physician leader, involved. In my experience, physicians respond more positively to a compliance message when another physician is involved.

Quick Tip: CMO

Build a strong relationship with your CMO. The CMO can be a critical ally for you when addressing identified physician clinical or behavioral concerns impacting the compliance program. Additionally, the CMO can serve as a physician champion to help promote the compliance program to all physicians on the medical staff.

Note: While the above discussion relates to a CMO role, the same can be applied to other types of physician leaders, such as medical staff leadership positions or medical directors.

Legal Counsel (e.g., General Counsel, Associate General Counsel, Outside Counsel)

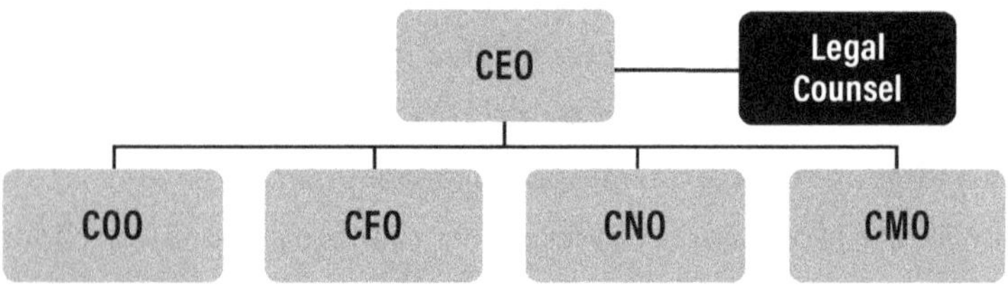

Up front, it should be noted that not every healthcare organization will have legal counsel on staff (generally referred to as "in-house counsel"). Organizations that do not employ legal counsel may contract out for legal services. Often, the determination for having in-house counsel boils down to a business decision from the CEO or board. The decision is shaped by factors such as the cost of employing counsel vs. contracting out and the volume of legal work needed for the organization. For those organizations that do employ legal counsel, depending on the size and scope of services provided, the legal department may consist of a single individual, or a staff of attorneys. Additionally, consider that even for organizations that have in-house counsel, the nature of certain legal work may still require a need for a specialized attorney (e.g., litigation, fraud and abuse, tax exemption, and bond financing).

Regardless of whether the attorneys are in-house or external, legal counsel has the overall role of a protecting the organization from corporate liability. It is important to note that the role of legal counsel is to serve the needs of their client, and that client is the organization. It is not you or other employees in the organization. While the exact responsibilities of legal counsel will vary by organization and individual skillset, their duties generally include the following:

- **Advising Leadership.** Advising the CEO, members of senior management, and the board on legal issues related to fraud and abuse, patient privacy, corporate liability, licensure and certification, scope of practice, and if applicable, tax exemption.

- **Contracts.** Reviewing and drafting all organizational contracts (e.g., physician contracts, equipment or space leases, supplier and vendor contracts, managed care contracts).
- **Corporate Legal Documents**. Reviewing and drafting all corporate legal documents (e.g., articles of organization or incorporation, operating agreements, shareholder agreements, and financial documents such as those related to loans or bond financing).
- **Governance Documents.** Reviewing and drafting all governance-related documents (e.g., board committee charters, board resolutions)
- **Legal Filings.** Ensuring any federal, state, or local legal documents are filed and kept up to date with the appropriate government agency (e.g., Internal Revenue Service, secretary of state, county planning office).
- **Registered Agent**. Serving as a registered agent for purposes of any federal, state, or local government filings or service of process for litigation purposes.
- **Government Agency Correspondence.** Responding to any court or government agency issued documents, visits or inquiries (e.g., court orders, criminal or civil subpoenas, audits, or requests for information)
- **Advising Internal Customers.** Serving as legal counsel to internal customers such as the human resources, compliance, IT, finance, and marketing departments.

- **Organizational compliance.** Ensuring the organization is maintaining compliance with all federal, state, and local laws and regulations as well as supporting a healthy culture of compliance.

In order to carry out these responsibilities, legal counsel must be licensed to practice law (through bar admission). Additionally, they must have excellent skills at written and verbal communication, negotiation, research, and conflict resolution.

Thinking like Legal Counsel

When it comes to your work as a compliance officer, be thinking about it from the perspective of legal counsel—that is, someone who is tasked with protecting the organization from liability. For these particular healthcare leaders, I want to pause and be clear. When I say to think about your work from the perspective of legal counsel, I am not saying you should give others a legal opinion or otherwise engage in conduct considered to be the practice of law. What I am saying is more simulated. Similar to the other healthcare leaders we've discussed, imagine you are in the position of legal counsel as you are viewing a problem you are working on. I'll give an example to help explain this point.

Imagine you have identified a situation involving clinical staff who have provided services to patients beyond what they were trained and licensed to provide under state law. As the compliance officer, your concerns may be related to compliance with federal and state licensure and training requirements, as well as inappropriately billing payers.

As legal counsel, those would also be concerns, but your focus is going to also be centered around liability—financial liability for repayments and potential fines and penalties. Additionally, you're going to be focused on liability from the perspective of patient care, potential harm to patients and the possibility of legal action and how to mitigate those risks. Finally, you are also going to be concerned about protecting communications about the matter before and after it was identified.

So with any compliance matter, be thinking about two things when it comes to communicating with legal counsel: first, identifying how legal counsel might view a concern from a liability standpoint, and second, what information legal needs in order to make a decision. Keep in mind that similar to compliance officers, legal counsel need to know the facts in order to give an opinion. Figure 4.6 includes a sample of typical political pressures for legal counsel that shape their POV.

Figure 4.6. Legal Counsel Political Pressures.

- The CEO and board expecting legal counsel to keep the organization protected from liability associated with violations of federal, state, and local laws
- The board, the CEO, or department directors expecting legal counsel to respond or turn around legal deliverables within short timeframes (e.g., legal opinions, contracts, amendments)
- The CFO expecting legal counsel to keep any operating or liability-related expenses within budget
- The CMO and CEO expecting legal counsel to accommodate financial transactions or clinical peer review needs in order to resolve conflict involving a physician
- The government expecting legal counsel to ensure accurate responses to any government agency-related activities (e.g., federal or state law filings, litigation, audits, requests for information)
- The applicable bar association expecting legal counsel not to engage in conduct that would jeopardize his or her ability to practice law
- The government and the compliance officer expecting legal counsel to ensure the organization remains compliant with all laws and regulations

Positioning compliance for Legal Counsel's POV

The POV of a legal counsel is going to be shaped by several self-interests, some of which we've discussed with other leaders. First, what is in the best interest of the patient? Here, the focus will be on what can we do as an organization to avoid harm to the patient, or with instances that did harm a patient, prevent it from happening in the future. Second, what is in the best interest of the organization? Here, legal counsel's focus will be protecting or reducing the organization's exposure to liability. That means advising against conduct that will create liability and taking steps to correct conduct that has created liability. Finally, what is in the best interest of legal counsel from a professional standards standpoint? As licensed attorneys, legal counsel must abide by certain professional conduct standards established by the bar associations that govern their practice. As legal counsel, with knowledge of certain conduct, this individual will be motivated to ensure that whatever actions or decisions are taken do not jeopardize counsel's ability to do his or her job in a professional manner. For example, this could be demonstrated by giving bad advice, taking sides in a situation that requires neutrality, or violating a patient or employee's privacy.

Quick Tip: Legal Counsel

Build a strong relationship with your legal counsel. As an individual with oversight for the organization from a liability standpoint, legal counsel will become a significant business partner for you in identifying and resolving potential compliance issues. For example, he or she can advise on potential violations of law, offer guidance on how best to resolve a matter, or protect certain documents from disclosure.

Department Leadership (Administrative or Clinical)

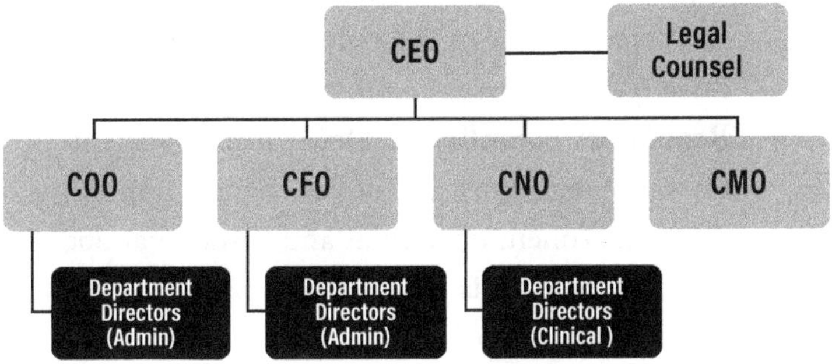

Finally, we have the department leaders, both on the administrative and clinical sides of the organization. Generally speaking, this group will have oversight into various operational departments and report up to one of the other senior leadership positions discussed earlier. While it would be impractical to cover every type of department leader, some common department leader positions are managers or supervisors over patient care departments, and administrative managers or supervisors over registration, scheduling, billing, coding, health information management, and case management. Most department leaders have responsibilities that include the following:

- **Departmental processes.** Department leaders oversee the departments' processes to ensure efficiency, compliance, and quality.
- **Staff supervision.** Department leaders supervise various staff to carry out departmental functions.

- **Financial management.** These leaders manage departmental finances, including managing budgets and expenses as well as developing opportunities to drive revenue.
- **Regulatory compliance.** Department leaders stay on top of regulatory and policy changes impacting their department operations and ensure that operations are in compliance.

Thinking Like a Department Leader

The POV of a departmental leader is shaped by three self-interests. First, what is in the best interest of the patient? Regardless of whether the leader is on the clinical or administrative side of healthcare, department leaders know the patient is at the top of the organizational chart. These leaders will be motivated to ensure their staff provide excellent customer service and their patients receive high quality care. Second, what is in the best interest of the organization? Departmental leaders have budgetary and HR responsibilities within the organization that must be met. As leaders who report up to senior management, department leaders will be motivated by what supports their leaders and the organization in meeting its performance goals. Finally, what is in the best interest of the department? As spokespeople for the department, these leaders will be looking out for the best interests of their staff. Figure 4.7 includes a sample of typical political pressures department leaders face that shape their POV.

Figure 4.7. Department Leader Political Pressures

- The CEO and other senior management expecting all department leaders to meet identified business and performance goals
- The CEO and other senior management expecting the clinical department leaders to deliver high-quality care to patients
- The CEO and other senior management expecting all clinical department leaders to keep patients safe and resolve identified clinical risk concerns
- The physicians expecting all clinical department leaders to resolve workflow issues affecting patient care
- The CEO and other senior management expecting all clinical department leaders to meet quality standards tied to reimbursement
- The CEO/board expecting all department leaders to successfully pass organizational surveys and inspections
- The CFO expecting all department leaders to meet operational budget goals and do more with less
- Department employees expecting the department leader to keep up with the staffing, equipment, and technology resources of the organization's competitors
- The government and the compliance officer expecting the department leaders to ensure the organization remains compliant with all laws and regulations

Positioning Compliance for a Department Leader's POV

When it comes to your work as a compliance officer, be thinking about it from the department leader's perspective.

If you were this department leader, what information would you want to know? Typically, when it comes to department leaders, they are going to view whatever you have to say from the lens of how it impacts their department's operations and staff. For that reason, be mindful of their role as a leader over the staff in their department, the fact the department leader has budgetary and HR responsibilities, and whom they report to at the senior leadership level.

Quick Tip: Department Leaders

Build a strong relationship with your administrative and clinical department directors. These folks will become significant assets to your compliance programs. Since they are closest to daily work involved in the organization's operations, they can provide feedback and support for investigations or how a regulatory change is going to impact operations.

Pulling it All Together

Knowing how to think like the healthcare leaders covered in chapters three and four is important to navigating the politics of healthcare. It puts you in a position to identify *the why* behind certain questions they're asking you and decisions they make. Also, you will be better equipped to be empathetic to their challenges. Finally, it helps you relate to your audience, which is important when you are communicating with them or trying to better understand the politics involved in the business decisions they are making.

With each healthcare leader I covered over the course of the last two chapters you likely noticed a pattern forming with the quick tips—building strong relationships. In the next chapter, we're going to explore how to do just that.

Chapter Takeaways

- The CNO, Legal Counsel, CMO, and department leaders have a particular POV which shapes their individual self-interests.
- Knowing how to think like a healthcare leader means you understand the leader's role and responsibilities, their political pressures, as well as how to position compliance to appeal to their particular POV.
- When you think like a healthcare leader you improve your ability to communicate your compliance message to your audience and gain buy-in to the compliance program.

Chapter Five

Building Strong Relationships with Healthcare Leaders

I've learned that people will forget what you said, people will forget what you did, but people will never forget how you made them feel.

—Maya Angelou

Top Five Defensive Leader Comments

1. "Are you crazy? You want us to do what?"
2. "We've always done it this way…"
3. "You just don't know operations…"
4. "You're just an obstacle to me getting s*** done."
5. "Do you know what the _____ I do for a living?"

Assume you are the compliance officer for a physician-owned entity, such as a large physician practice. The Centers for Medicare and Medicaid Services (CMS) just issued new final regulations directly affecting your organization's operations. You are sitting in a board meeting explaining the new regulations and how they will affect the organization. Right in the middle of your presentation, the physician board chair interrupts you and says, "Do you know what the F**k we do for a living?" An awkward silence then fills the room as if two parents were arguing in front of their children.

If you haven't experienced it yet, there will come a time when a healthcare leader confronts you about a compliance program initiative in a less-than-flattering way. A close friend of mine used to call such interactions "self-esteem workshops."

Kidding aside, while these events are not super fun, they do need to be viewed as growth moments. Just keep in mind they are driven by the POV and political pressure discussion I outlined in chapters three and four. Over the course of my career, I have experienced many of these self-esteem workshops, including a situation very similar to the one I described above.

One of the biggest hurdles you will constantly face in your career is getting buy-in to the compliance program from the leaders in your organization. A common challenge in this profession is leaders resistant to the work you do, either due to defensiveness or disengagement. Though your job is not to become their BFF, it is to operate a successful compliance program, which depends heavily upon leaders being engaged to a culture of compliance. This is an example of where the politics of healthcare will collide with your role. In order to operate an effective compliance program, you have to develop strong relationships with your leaders, which will require a little politicking of your own.

So how do you build strong relationships with leaders—even the pain-in-the-a** ones? Three strategies that have helped me are (1) establishing rapport with leaders, (2) building and maintaining trust with leaders, and (3) supporting leaders by being a business partner. Let's walk through these in more detail.

Establishing Rapport with Leaders

Establishing rapport is going to be your starting point for building strong relationships with leaders. While there are endless ways in which you can establish rapport with a leader, two specific approaches that have helped me over the years include (1) knowing the organization's market, and (2) taking an active interest in my leaders.

Knowing the Organization's Market

As part of onboarding with any organization, something I have always done is carve out time to research the organization and the market in which it participates. For example, if I worked for a health system, I would research the organization's history, including recent expansions of any service lines as well as mergers or partnerships with other market participants. Some of this work you may have done as part of applying for the job, but this will be a time to take a deeper dive and review documents you would otherwise not have access to as an outsider. Figure 5.1 includes some tips for getting to know your organization's market.

Figure 5.1. Knowing the Market Tips

- **Set aside time.** Designate a certain time each day or during the week to read articles and other information targeted at the local and national markets in which your organization participates.
- **Stay current on the market.** Subscribe to free healthcare market news services that provide news relevant to your organization's market. You can also scan national and local news agencies for stories on your market.
- **Seek leader insight.** Ask your leaders where they get their market information, and see if they will share their resources with you (hint: you may find the organization has a subscription to some media services).
- **Be observant.** Pay attention to comments made in meetings. Often you will pick up information from leaders about what is taking place in your market or nationally.
- **Conduct targeted market research.** Visit the websites or social media sites of competitors in your market. Often their marketing or PR department will post information about new service lines or business initiatives.
- **Set up search engine alerts.** If there is activity with a competitor you want to track in the news, set up a search engine alert (e.g., Google alert).

If you take the time to do your homework on your organization's market, it will help you initiate or engage in discussions with leaders about the market. When you know your market, it sends a strong message to your leaders that you are engaged in their work. When you are engaged in their work, it demonstrates empathy, which helps establish rapport. In my experience, I have found that when you are engaged with leaders in their work, they are more likely to reciprocate by being engaged in yours. They may not want to talk endlessly about sampling and extrapolation methodologies when conducting audits, but you will see them proactively reach out with identified concerns.

Bonus material: For additional tips on how to establish rapport with your leaders, visit my Establishing Rapport Tips sheet at: http://www.bluebirdhealthlaw.com/book-bonuses.

Take an Active Interest in Leaders

Another strategy that has helped me in establishing rapport is taking an active interest in my leaders. Recall that in chapter two, I mentioned the meet and greet in the context of identifying key leaders. Aside from the benefits I've already mentioned, these meetings are an excellent first step toward demonstrating an active interest in your leaders. This is especially true if you are the one who initiates that meeting. As you are meeting with your leaders, find out as much as you can about them professionally. For example, you could ask questions such as the following:

- How long have you been in healthcare?
- Did you experience a career change?

- How long have you been with the organization?
- What responsibilities do you have?
- What does your day, week, or month look like?
- How many direct reports do you have?
- To whom do you report?

These are just some examples of the types of questions you can explore. The overall mindset should be one of curiosity. The more you come across as curious, the less you will come across as judgmental. By diving into some of these questions, you will not only expand your knowledge but also demonstrate an active interest in your leaders.

Another approach is to have them walk you through their roles, responsibilities, or departments. People love to talk about themselves and take pride in what they have accomplished. Since you're not the leader's significant other, chances are they will just be thrilled that someone wants to hear them talk about their job. Aside from a sit-down discussion about the work they do, ask to shadow their staff or have them lead you on a department walkthrough. It will send a message to the leader you are genuinely interested in the work they do. In the end they will appreciate that you took the time to learn their operations and understand the challenges from their perspective. Taking these steps will demonstrate empathy, which will help build rapport. Over time, this work will pay off when the leader comes back to you with a compliance issue to resolve.

These meetings can also be opportunities to find out as much as you can personally about your leaders. Now obviously there is a fine line to your inquiries. You don't want to get too personal—or, you know, HR will want to have a little chat. Here, to keep from getting too personal, focus on *their story*. Everyone has a story about how they got into whatever it is they do. You heard about mine back at the beginning of this book. Since asking, "Hey, man. What's your story?" is not super graceful, here are some more respectful ways to approach asking about their story:

- How did you get into this line of work?
- What has been your biggest accomplishment so far?
- What do you like to do when you are not working?
- What's your favorite movie?
- What's your favorite restaurant?
- What do you miss about living in [insert city, town, state, or country]?
- If you could go anywhere in the world right now, where would it be?
- If you could go back and relive one famous moment in time, what would it be?
- Who is the most famous person you've met?

When you dive into a healthcare leader's story, you gain insight and perspective into who they are as a person. Did they experience a career change late in life? Did they relocate for this job? Was there a single event that led them into healthcare? I once worked with a nurse leader who had a younger sister diagnosed with a terminal illness as a child. Taking care of her sister is what led her to becoming a nurse. That was over twenty years ago, and I can still remember her story. I can recall the time of year we chatted and even the room we were sitting in!

Whatever your leader's story is, identifying it creates an opportunity for building rapport. When you take the time to learn about a leader personally, you are demonstrating an active interest in them. These efforts will establish a meaningful connection with your leaders, which helps strengthen your relationship with them. Figure 5.2 includes some additional tips for demonstrating an active interest in your healthcare leaders.

Figure 5.2. Active Interest Tips

1. Notice and acknowledge them in individual or group settings.
2. Share news stories or other items of interest specific to their roles.
3. Ask them questions to get them to talk about themselves and what they like.
4. Listen to their stories or points of view with curiosity, not judgment.
5. Ask for their input during times when you're not working on something together.

Establishing rapport with leaders will not happen overnight. You truly need to approach it as one step at a time, meaning one interaction at a time. The more curiosity conversations you start, though, the better you will become at them.

Quick Tip: Establishing Rapport with Leaders

Study a map. One of the easiest ways to build a connection and show interest in someone else is to talk about where that person is from or where they lived at some point. Even if you're not from that location or haven't lived there, studying a map will give you a foundation of knowledge to strike up a conversation.

Building and Maintaining Trust with Leaders

Another approach for developing strong relationships with leaders is building *and maintaining* trust with them. Like any relationship, whether personal or professional, trust has to be earned over time and must be evidenced by actions, not words. I tend to think of trust as a form of currency. Like currency, it takes time to build it up, but if you are not careful, it can be squandered pretty quickly. Below are some specific strategies for building and maintaining trust that have helped me over the years.

Honest Communication

Whether you're responding to a question being asked or promising a deliverable by a certain date, be honest in your communication with leaders. This is crucial especially during times when the content of your communication is less than desirable. Let's take a look at a couple of common scenarios in which you can get into trouble with leaders if you were not being honest in your communication.

The first one is when a compliance officer is asked a question that he or she doesn't know the answer to at the time the question is asked. If you are faced with this scenario, don't make up an answer based on assumptions and educated guesses. You will gain more trust and respect if you are transparent by telling them you don't know the answer to their question. If you try to schmooze your way through a response, (a) it's going be obvious to everyone involved, *except you*, and (b) if you're wrong, you're going to have to circle back and explain that you were wrong. That's not going be a fun conversation for you. It also may cause leaders to question trusting you and your competence.

For whatever reason many new compliance officers put a lot of pressure on themselves to always know an answer and feel insecure if they reveal to others that they don't know an answer. This profession is a practice, and there is nothing wrong with not knowing an answer. You just need to make sure your leaders can feel confident you will obtain the answer. So in this situation, honest communication looks something like saying, "I don't know the answer, but I will find out and get back to you." Just make sure you do follow up. If you don't, your communication will shift from honest to dishonest, and you'll lose their trust.

Another common source of dishonest communication relates to deadlines. When it comes to communicating with leaders about deadlines, there are a few variations on this communication that can get you in trouble if you're not careful. The first is not communicating with leaders when it becomes apparent to you a deadline is going to be missed. If you know you are not going to make the deadline, proactively communicate that fact to your leaders, along with the reason for the delay.

The second variation, sometimes connected to the first one, is dishonesty about the reason for the delay. If the reason is you, don't make excuses or blame someone else. Be up front with your leaders by taking ownership for the delay. "I know I owe you an answer on ______. I'm sorry for the delay. That was my fault." You don't need to go into any further explanation why, especially if it is going to sound like an excuse. Just apologize, take ownership, and communicate when they can expect a response. In my experience, I have found that while healthcare leaders may not be happy to miss the deadline, they will appreciate you being honest with them.

The third variation on honest communication about deadlines relates to competing demands on your time. You will almost always have competing priorities, so proactively disclose them so you can mutually establish a reasonable deadline. Your leader likely is not going to be aware of your competing priorities, so it's partly to make them aware but also for them to make you aware of their deadlines for a decision. Leaders love to come to you with a question or issue they claim is urgent but then fail to communicate a specific deadline. They'll say something like, "I need this as soon as possible." Now I don't know about you, but the last time I checked, "as soon as possible" isn't actually a date on the calendar. So take the time to proactively communicate competing priorities and find out specifically when they actually need an answer.

Meet Your Deadlines

Sticking with the topic of deadlines, actually meeting them when you said you would can be a whole other challenge to maintaining trust with leaders. There will be times when the uncertain nature of your work will create a circumstance beyond your control such that you miss a deadline. For example, on Monday afternoon you get contacted by a leader with a question requiring research, and you make a promise to respond with an answer by Wednesday. The next morning the CEO contacts you because some government surveyors have shown up responding to a patient complaint. As healthcare industry workers, leaders function on a daily basis in an uncertain world, so they know unexpected conflicts will come up.

A challenge that some people have when it comes to failing to meet a deadline is not being honest with themselves about their current workload. When it comes to deadlines, it is best to err on the side of under promising and overdelivering instead of the other way around. So be honest about when you can *reasonably* expect to complete the work. With any compliance issue, you likely will face three challenges to your time:

1. Other issues of equal priority
2. Unexpected issues arising (e.g., government investigation)
3. Unknown variables in researching an issue (i.e., when you're researching an answer and several other questions surface that must be answered too)

Factoring in the above, do you have a reasonable amount of time to complete the work, or are you going to have to pull an all-nighter? If you're not honest with yourself, it will become apparent to your leaders, who may question whether you're being honest with them.

Be Consistent in the Approach to Your Work

A significant way to build trust is to be consistent in how you approach your work, whether you are consulting on a project, conducting an investigation, or anything in between. If you're not aware of this, you will find that leaders do not like surprises. When you are inconsistent in approach, leaders feel uncertain about what to expect from you, which creates a feeling of potentially being surprised. When you are consistent, leaders feel certain about what to expect, which in turns helps build trust.

While the above approaches are not intended to be an all-inclusive list, they do hit on key sources of mistrust by healthcare leaders in the daily life of a compliance officer. For that reason, be mindful of how you are performing in these areas in order to maintain trust with your leaders.

Quick Tip: Building and Maintaining Trust with Leaders

Avoid negative politics. A key way to help build and maintain trust is to avoid engaging in negative politics such as spreading rumors, gossiping, or passing judgment on others. I'm not suggesting that you not voice objections or criticism—just make sure that when you do, it's from an organizational perspective—not a personal one.

Supporting Leaders by Being a Business Partner

Another effective strategy for building strong relationships with leaders is supporting them by being a business partner. To be clear, by being a business partner, I am saying to treat your role as a value-added resource to help your leaders in making their business decisions. I am not suggesting you allow them to make whatever decisions they want without pushback or objection. Similar to a CFO who is consulted when financial analysis is needed, as the compliance officer, you should view your role in the same way. And like a CFO, there is an expectation to deliver both the good news and bad news. Your approach should be no different. While there are a number of different ways you can demonstrate business partnership to your leaders, below are three specific approaches that have helped me over the years.

Think "Efficiency" When Interacting with Your Leaders

On a daily basis, healthcare leaders are constantly challenged by time and their attention being pulled in multiple directions. If you want to experience the daily life of a healthcare leader, shadow one for a day if they'll let you. When it comes to business partnership, being mindful of how efficient you can be in the approach to your work will help support them. Let me give you a couple of examples to help illustrate how this plays out.

First, let's assume you are planning a meeting to discuss a complex issue, one involving multiple departments, and maybe multiple software programs too. For discussion sake, we'll also throw in some specific billing and coding rules that have to be followed. Before this meeting occurs, communicate with your audience. Let them know the purpose of the meeting, and give them the relevant history and background they need to know in their role in order to make a decision. Going through this process will enable a smoother discussion because everyone will be up to speed before the meeting begins. Also, some leaders are "thinkers" or "analyzers," and this approach gives them the opportunity to think about the discussion and identify whether others need to be involved in the discussion. That reduces the chances of scheduling a follow-up meeting that could have been avoided. So be thinking about how efficient you can be when it comes to meetings.

Another example of efficiency is to make sure you are prepared when you do meet. If the meeting is related to discussing policies or contracts, make sure that you have done your research to answer questions that likely will come up. Additionally, make sure you have copies at the ready to produce if those documents need to be reviewed in the meeting. If there are specific sections within certain documents that will be discussed, make sure you can go to these sections quickly (e.g., highlight or dog-ear). Fumbling around to find information is a strong indicator of not being prepared for the discussion, which is not being efficient with a leader's time.

Another example, one that is connected to the first two, is anticipating their questions and being prepared with answers. If you are encountering an issue for the first time and you are not sure of the questions you may get asked, then run your scenario by a trusted colleague or your supervisor. They may be an invaluable resource to help you spot potential questions you will get asked. While you can't predict with 100 percent certainty, if you are thinking from the POV of your audience, you should be able to anticipate some of the questions they may ask you.

Finally, another example of efficiency, is making information such that it is *easy to find and access.* For example, let's say you are being asked a policy-related question about the verification of identity under your organization's privacy policies. In the past I have experienced a number of newer compliance officers who would copy and paste part of the policy that presumably answers the question and send it to a leader. There was no explanation or analysis given, and no frame of reference as to where in the policy this information can be found. Don't do that. Instead, clearly identify the information to your leader. You want to explain what the answer is, and end your communication by telling them where the answer can be found (e.g., "See the bottom of page 7, under Section III A [1][c]."). Presenting information in such a way that it is easy to find and digest demonstrates efficiency, which will be well received by your healthcare leaders.

Explain "the Why"

Another significant way you can support your leaders by being a business partner is to explain *the why* behind your answers. In my example above related to making information easy to find, I have also experienced a lot of newer compliance officers who don't take the extra time needed to explain their answers. When that happens, it opens up opportunities for misunderstandings or incorrect information. Leaders are not as close to the regulations as you are, so you need to take the extra time needed to explain answers to them in order to help them understand.

Recognize Leaders and Employees When They Support You

Another approach for supporting your leaders by being a business partner is to recognize them or their direct reports when they have supported the compliance program. For example, let's assume you work as a compliance officer in a hospital. One day, the lab director walks into your office and hands you some discharge instructions she found sitting on a table out in the ED waiting room. The lab director says, "I found these sitting out. I'm not sure where they go but wanted to make sure they didn't end up in the trash."

In this scenario, after conducting the necessary risk assessment, if it were me, I would take the time to send that lab director a handwritten thank-you note. I would let her know how much I appreciated her efforts to take the time to make sure the information got to a safe place to prevent a potential breach. I would also reinforce the fact that because I cannot be everywhere at all times, it takes employees like her to ensure the success of our compliance program. Sending such a note is not trying to be the lab director's bestie; rather, it is recognizing her support of the compliance program. It also encourages her to continue to support the program and model that behavior to her employees.

A big challenge we all face in this role is getting people to speak up about reporting concerns. Taking the time to recognize such efforts helps improve a culture of compliance. In the above example, if I wanted to take it a step further, I might send a similar note to the lab director's supervisor requesting that she be appropriately recognized. Figure 5.4. provides some additional tips for supporting your leaders.

Figure 5.4. Supporting Leader Tips

1. Present information in a manner that is easy to understand by using relatable examples.
2. See the matter you are working on from the perspective of the healthcare leader (i.e., understand their POV).
3. Always be mindful of a potential knowledge gap between you and the leader about a compliance requirement.
4. Recognize their special events or days (e.g., birthdays, accomplishments, doctors' day, nurses' week).
5. Show up and be engaged for their meetings.

Supporting your leaders is not about playing favorites; it is about demonstrating respect so that it provides an opportunity to be reciprocated. Keep in mind that it will be an investment in your time and effort, beyond your normal duties. If you put in the energy, though, you will experience a return on that investment in the form of leaders engaged with your compliance program.

Quick Tip: Supporting Leaders

Support your leaders when they need it most. If you sense a leader is in a vulnerable operational position (e.g., short-staffed), support them by being flexible with any work they may owe you. When you do, they will return the favor in supporting your compliance program. Strong relationships are built on reciprocity.

Bonus material: For additional tips on how to support your leaders, visit my Supporting Healthcare Leader Tips sheet at: http://www.bluebirdhealthlaw.com/book-bonuses.

Pulling it All Together

Building strong relationships with your leaders is a critical strategy to navigating the politics of healthcare. In my experience, others will see you as someone they can trust, someone who can follow through with commitments and keep confidential information…well, confidential. If you put forth the time and effort, strong relationships can help provide many benefits. For example, you can gain access to information you might not otherwise be able to obtain. Strong relationships also create trusted resources with whom you can discuss difficult situations and from whom you can obtain honest feedback.

Building strong relationships with leaders also helps you gain buy-in to the compliance program. At the beginning of this chapter, I mentioned a circumstance I encountered with a defensive physician several years ago. By deploying the above strategies, I was able to turn that relationship around over the course of a few months. Eventually, he started reaching out to me, instead of the other way around. So in that regard, you are not only building strong relationships with leaders, but you are also building compliance partners to support your program.

Now that we have talked about building strong relationships with your healthcare leaders, let's talk about how to use diplomacy to effectively communicate with them. That will be our focus in the next chapter.

Chapter Takeaways

- Some healthcare leaders will be engaged in compliance, while others will not.
- Regardless of a leader's engagement with compliance, successfully navigating the politics of healthcare requires building strong relationships with them.
- Three ways to build strong relationships with your leaders include 1) establishing rapport, 2) building and maintaining trust, and 3) supporting your leaders.
- Building strong relationships with leaders takes time and often requires you to have patience while putting in time and effort.

Chapter Six

Using Diplomacy to Influence Behavior

A diplomat is a man who always remembers a woman's birthday, but never remembers her age.
—Robert Frost

Imagine you're the compliance officer for XYZ, P.C. (XYZ), a physician practice. CMS has just passed a new regulation impacting how the practice provides a particular professional service. The new rules take effect in ninety days. In order to ensure the practice remains compliant after the changes take effect, you'll need to assess XYZ's current operations. You'll also need to oversee an action plan involving multiple departments to ensure their existing procedures come into compliance. These particular changes will impact multiple department managers who have historically not gotten along. They also have been resistant to compliance. How will you go about bringing these individuals together to successfully implement the new changes within the next ninety days?

From conducting investigations to advising leadership to educating staff, compliance officers are continually placed in a position to influence the actions of others. If you want to navigate the politics of healthcare successfully, and gain buy-in to your compliance program, you'll need a diplomatic approach for influencing others' behavior.

For purposes of discussion, I define "diplomacy" as the ability to assert your ideas and opinions in a manner that is respectful of all parties involved. Being diplomatic means you are able to maintain a balance of neutral positioning while being skilled at negotiation and persuasion. In order to achieve that balance, you have to actively listen to others, know when it is appropriate to assert your opinions, and know when to exercise self-control. Piggybacking off our discussion in chapters three and four, diplomacy also requires that you understand others' POVs. In this chapter, we will take a focused look at diplomacy related to those POVs as another strategy for navigating the politics of healthcare.

How to Diplomatically Communicate

At the center of diplomacy *is communication*—more specifically, how you interact with others and how you communicate your message. Specific to the compliance program's agenda, that message is typically "Do this" or "Don't do this," both of which are focused on influencing the actions of others.

An unfortunate reality of our profession that affects influencing the actions of others is the perception of compliance officers. Before you even have a chance to utter a single word, healthcare leaders will see you as an obstacle—some sort of grown-up version of a hall monitor. That doesn't mean the perception can't be overcome; you just need to put in some effort to change how they see your role in the organization. If you carry out the strategies covered in this book, over time you will experience this perception change to that of a business partner. As it relates to diplomatic communications, being self-aware about how you are delivering your compliance message helps change the perception of compliance. Below are some approaches that have helped me over the years to ensure my message was being delivered in a diplomatic manner.

Know Your Audience

A key component of diplomatic communication is knowing your audience. If you are communicating a message, but the audience is not able to connect with it, do they really understand what you're saying? Knowing your audience doesn't mean completely changing your message, but rather altering it so that your audience understands. Keep in mind that most healthcare organizations contain employees of varying demographic, educational, and professional backgrounds. For that reason, you need to take these differences into account when you are delivering your compliance message.

When it comes to communicating to different audiences, the compliance message of "Do this" or "Don't do this" doesn't vary, but *how* you communicate the message will. This is where the concept of relatable examples, tailored to the audience, comes into play. For example, if I were educating a nursing unit about HIPAA and safeguarding protected patient health information (PHI), I would use an example common to the nursing profession—thank-you notes from a patient. I would point out that when they receive a patient thank-you note, technically the note is PHI, which must be safeguarded. Alternatively, if I were educating a group of physicians about HIPAA and safeguarding PHI, I might use an example of discussing a patient's treatment plan in front of friends or family members. Any time you can use relatable examples, it will demonstrate knowing your audience.

If you want to know your audience, the first step is identifying who your audience is. Now, you may be thinking "Well no sh**t.", but there are times when the audience isn't readily apparent. For example, assume you work in a hospital and the ED director contacts you asking you to give an EMTALA[7] refresher training to "the clinical staff" in the ED. Ok, well who are the clinical staff? Is that nurses? Are paramedics included? Are ED, on-call physicians, or both included? What about nurse practitioners or physician assistants? In a situation like this, you call this out in order to determine exactly who will be your audience. Having this information helps ensure you can provide relatable examples as part of your training.

When it comes to knowing your audience, always approach the compliance message with consideration of the audience's POV. How would [insert your audience] view this particular topic? What questions would they have? What are some examples of work they perform on a daily basis? If you are not sure of the answers to these questions, ask the staff or the leaders over the staff. You then need to identify the takeaway points. What do you want this particular audience to walk away knowing about your message? I've said a lot here, so Figure 6.1 includes an simplified checklist to help you in knowing your audience.

Figure 6.1. Steps for Knowing Your Audience

- Step one: Identify your audience.
- Step two: Identify their POV and likely questions.
- Step three: Identify the takeaway points for this audience.

Knowing your audience is key to diplomatic communications. It helps ensure the information is delivered in a manner the audience can relate to. When your audience can relate to the information you are providing, it aids in their overall comprehension and retention of the message. Your audience will also feel like you understand *their* world, which in turn helps you obtain their buy-in to your world—the compliance program.

Quick Tip: Know Your Audience

Think like a Healthcare Leader, Not a Compliance Officer. A great way to demonstrate knowing your audience is to think like a healthcare leader and not a compliance officer as you are trying to diplomatically communicate.

Actively Listen

Another key component to diplomatic communication is active listening. Actively listening means you are fully engaged in the discussion you are participating in with others. When you are actively listening, you are hearing *what* the person is saying and *how* they are saying it.

In order to actively listen, your mind needs to be free from distraction (which means no multitasking) and receiving the information without judgment. Also, you need to show respect toward the speaker by making eye contact and not interrupting or rushing the conversation. Be present and in the moment. Additionally, there are some approaches you can use to demonstrate active listening. First, when there is a natural pause in the discussion, you can ask questions to confirm you are understanding the information. You can also "speak back" or regurgitate the information to the speaker to validate that you understand. This confirms to both you and the speaker that you understand the information he or she is conveying. Figure 6.2 includes some additional helpful tips for active listening.

Figure 6.2. Active Listening Tips

- Eliminate your distractions (mental and physical).
- Minimize murmurs when responding ("uh huh," "um hmm") and respond with questions ("So what happened next?").
- Ask clarifying questions ("So let me make sure I'm understanding this correctly…").
- Avoid one-upping ("This reminds me of a time that…").
- Don't interrupt the speaker with proposed solutions.

Actively listening is critical to diplomatic communications because it sends a message to the other person that what he or she is saying is valued. Taking this approach will ensure they feel heard, which can be the underlying message to a compliance concern when it is raised. In order to actively listen, you need to have both a genuine desire to understand the information being presented to you and offer support to the speaker.

Quick Tip: Actively Listening

Focus on Curiosity. To help stay engaged in the conversation, focus on being curious about what the other person is saying.

Exercise Self-Control

Depending upon the facts and circumstances of the matter and with whom the matter is being discussed, a diplomatic approach may require exercising self-control. For example, if the concern is on a need-to-know basis, and there are individuals present outside that category, it may be best to hold a separate discussion offline from the larger group and circle back as needed. Taking this approach can be beneficial for all parties involved in the need-to-know circle. It ensures that everyone feels comfortable that the matter is being discussed with the appropriate individuals, and you're able to resolve the concern without unnecessarily alarming others. If an analogy will help, think of this scenario akin to a physician needing to discuss a patient's condition with the patient, but other individuals unknown to the physician are also in the room.

Another common scenario requiring the exercise of self-control is when someone unexpectedly mentions business conduct taking place that may not be compliant. You'll see this periodically happen during a meeting. In these situations, often you are only hearing a limited set of facts but you need to obtain more information before making a decision. Exercising self-control may be necessary to avoid setting off a false alarm or embarrassing the person who spoke up. If you exercise self-control, you have the ability to further research the matter in order to reach a conclusion. You can then communicate the concern and planned course of action to correct.

Related to both scenarios, if you feel your concerns need to be voiced in the moment, here is another diplomatic approach. Label the concern as a *potential* concern but one that you need to further investigate in order to make a determination. This allows you to voice your concern but to leave the door open as to which way the answer will end up. If you do take this approach, just make sure you report back to the group.

Self-control requires practice. To help guide you in determining whether to exercise self-control, here are three questions you can ask yourself:

1. Does this need to be said?
2. Does this need to be said by me?
3. Does this need to be said now?

If you can answer "yes" to all three questions, then you know it's best to proceed. On the other hand, if you are hesitant with any one of the questions, then self-control is required. Most of the time, you can easily get through questions 1 and 2. It is number 3 that tends to cause hesitation—for example, if you are given limited facts and need time to investigate or if the topic is political because of certain self-interests from those involved.

Exercising self-control is about leveraging the timing of your communications. There may be certain times when raising a concern in the moment is appropriate, while at other times, it is better to hold off. To be effective at diplomatically influencing behavior, your timing has to be adaptable to the circumstances of your particular situation.

Quick Tip: Exercising Self-Control

Consider Time, Place, and Manner. When determining whether to exercise self-control, think about time, place, and manner. Is this the time to say something? Is this the physical place to say something? What is the best manner for saying something (e.g., in-person, email)?

Avoid Jumping to Conclusions

Another component of diplomatic communication is not jumping to conclusions before you have obtained and analyzed all the facts. For purposes of discussion here, jumping to conclusions means making assumptions based on incomplete facts. For example, let's assume you have oversight for HIPAA in your organization. A department director reports that an employee has snooped into the medical record of a coworker. At this particular point in time, you don't have all the facts to reasonably conclude whether or not a violation occurred. To that end, you don't want to label the allegation conclusively as a HIPAA violation until you have the facts to establish it. Instead, an incident like this should be referred to as "an alleged HIPAA violation" or a "potential HIPAA violation." These labels should remain in your communication until you reach the point of making a formal determination about the incident.

If you jump to conclusions, there are a couple of ramifications that can arise. First, there is potential you were led to a wrong conclusion. This can create confusion if you have to circle back and communicate a different conclusion to your audience. While everyone makes mistakes from time to time, you don't want this to become a pattern. If this becomes a pattern, your leaders may begin to lose trust and confidence in you. Additionally, it can create conflict or confusion with others who may have drawn a different conclusion. Another ramification can arise if you jump to a conclusion by labeling conduct as a violation prematurely. It can create an environment of unnecessary heightened risk, akin to shouting "Fire!" in a crowded theater. Make sure that before any official conclusions are made, your opinion is based on a thorough and comprehensive review of the facts.

In today's fast-paced working environment, there can be pressure to act quickly rather than spend the time needed to analyze the facts and requirements. Being able to make inferences based on available information is a key skill for any compliance officer, but you have to be careful not to make conclusions based on inferences alone. Conclusions have to be supported by verifiable facts.

Quick Tip: Avoid Jumping to Conclusions

Focus on Conclusions Supported by Facts. One way to ensure you're not jumping to conclusions is to run through a mental test by asking yourself: "Is my conclusion supported by facts that can be verified or my opinion?"

Vet the Accuracy of your Communication

Another component of diplomatic communication is vetting what you are saying to your audience for accuracy. To be clear, I'm not suggesting that all your communications need to be vetted. For example, if a coworker asks you the date for the upcoming holiday party and you get it wrong—that's probably not going to end your career. What I'm talking about are the communications that involve a higher level of risk. Let me give you three common examples to help illustrate the types of communications you want to vet for accuracy.

- Any communications with an external party, such as a patient/family member, government agency, organizational business partner, or the media.
- Any discussion with others inside the organization where you are analyzing or making a conclusion about a potential compliance concern.
- Any communications where you are providing an opinion that is interpreting a regulation, internal policy, or other formal guidance.

With these specific examples, there are some common denominators that signal a need to vet your communication. First, you could be discussing a matter of high risk to the organization. Second, you could be discussing a matter that is sensitive in nature (e.g., confidential, controversial, potential for conflict). Finally, you are communicating to an audience who is relying upon what you are saying, for purposes of making a significant business decision.

Regardless of circumstance, there will be times when it is critical to double or even triple check your facts. If you find yourself in a meeting, or another situation where you are having to verbally communicate about facts and you're not 100 percent sure, then let your audience know. Be transparent that you are not 100 percent certain of the facts and that you will verify and follow up. While vetting your communications does involve extra work, the time and energy spent will be less than the time it will take you to explain why your communication was originally inaccurate. Yes, we're all human, easily capable of mistakes. You just don't want to make it a practice. Taking the time to vet your communications will help guard against making inaccurate communications a practice.

Quick Tip: Vetting Your Communications

Use a Second Pair of Eyes for Written Communications. During times when you are drafting a written communication, have a trusted person look at it, such as a supervisor. Having this fresh perspective can help spot typos or identify any gaps in the communication or analysis that may raise a question.

Know the Organizational Chart and (as Needed) Leverage it for Support

Another component to diplomatic communication is knowing the organizational chart ("org chart") and leveraging it when you need to for support. This is true whether the org chart is within your department or across the organization.

What do I mean by *knowing* the org chart? As you are communicating with others on any compliance matter, you always want to be mindful of where your audience resides on the org chart. For example, there could be times when you get pulled into a discussion and not realize someone in your audience is at a higher level than you; or you may have thought you were communicating with an employee, but it turned out it was the employee's manager. I say these things as an individual speaking of mistakes that I made when I first started out.

Knowing the org chart means identifying where your audience sits before you attend a call or meeting. If that is not practical (e.g., someone attends without your prior knowledge), then be alert to the fact that you don't fully know your audience as you discuss the matter, and take steps to find out after the discussion. Knowing the org chart is important because it helps support some of the other diplomatic communication strategies, such as knowing your audience, exercising self-control, and vetting your communications.

Knowing the org chart can also be helpful for times when you need leverage. For example, let's assume you have an employee who has not responded to a request for documents or other information associated with an investigation or audit. As I mentioned in chapters one and two, there are individuals within your organization who have formal and informal power. When you know the org chart, you will know who has this power and therefore whom to go to for support when you need it.

Quick Tip: Know the Organizational Chart and (as Needed) Leverage It for Support

Make it a Habit. Before you attend a meeting or a call, make it a habit to spend time finding out who will be in attendance and identifying them on the org chart.

Communicating Diplomatically with Healthcare Leaders

When it comes to healthcare leaders, there are two considerations to keep in mind that impact how they communicate with you. The first is their education. Many leaders possess advanced degrees, such as MBAs, MPHs, JDs, or PhDs. That means they have been trained to be analytical in how they approach their decisions. In their professional lives, most healthcare leaders function through a groupthink model. For example, before a CEO will make a decision, he or she will have asked for input from various members of his or her leadership team. From the CEO's perspective, each stakeholder is responsible for providing input from their respective POV. The CEO will then take this input under advisement to help shape his or her decision.

When you combine all these characteristics together, healthcare leaders tend to think strategically with their decision making by considering multiple POVs. When you are communicating with healthcare leaders, you'll be more effective if you are mindful of this approach and apply it to how you approach your own work. When you do, your leaders will see you more like a business partner and less like an obstacle.

The second consideration to keep in mind is the fact that healthcare leaders are driven to be career oriented, which impacts how they make decisions politically. They view the business decisions they make as the steps along the way in a marathon, not a sprint. They put in long hours, often sacrificing their work-life balance in order to navigate political issues with physicians and other leaders. This is how they advance up the corporate ladder. As a result, healthcare leaders are savvy at operating with the big picture in mind—which is to say that they have a self-interest not to make political mistakes costing them their careers. For that reason, analyzing any compliance issue should take into account any political self-interests of those healthcare leaders involved.

When you communicate with your leaders, keep the considerations mentioned above in mind as you are interacting with them. In addition, below are some specific approaches that have helped me over the years.

Know How Decisions Are Made in the Organization

One way to communicate diplomatically with healthcare leaders about compliance matters is to demonstrate to them that you know how decisions are made in the organization. For example, if you are working on an issue that has a financial component to it, be mindful that a CEO will not make a decision unless the issue has been vetted by the CFO. So that means if you are meeting with the CEO to discuss the matter, you need to either invite the CFO to participate or, alternatively, let the CEO know you have already vetted the matter with the CFO. If taking the latter approach, you need to also be prepared to communicate what the CFO's response was and why. Taking this approach demonstrates to the CEO that you understand he or she won't make a decision without the CFO's input, and that you were prepared to address that concern. Knowing how decisions are made in the organization will help reduce any frustrations your leaders may have with you in operating inefficiently.

Quick Tip: Know How Decisions Are Made in the Organization

Think like a Healthcare Leader, not a Compliance Officer. I've said this a few times, but it is worth repeating here. If you think like a healthcare leader and not a compliance officer, it will help you identify what information a leader is going to need before making a decision.

When You Bring a Problem, Bring a Solution Too

If you have identified a compliance matter that needs to be addressed, make sure you are communicating the identified issue—and the proposed solution. For example, let's assume you have identified that an employee has snooped into the medical record of another employee. When you first alert your appropriate leader, explain what occurred but also the proposed steps to resolve the matter and prevent a future occurrence. As I've mentioned before, healthcare leaders do not like surprises, especially ones putting them and the organization at risk. When you take this approach, you will be reducing their anxiety by communicating a clear path for mitigating risk and restoring the organization back to a state of certainty.

Quick Tip: When You Bring a Problem, Bring a Solution Too

Apply to Supervisors. This approach should also be followed when communicating internally to your supervisor. When you propose a solution to an identified problem, it demonstrates your ability to independently think through the problem.

Mirror Their Communication Style

A significant way to communicate diplomatically with healthcare leaders is to mirror their communication styles. Everyone has a preferred communication style. If you don't know your leader's preferred style, then be observant of it and mirror it. In chapter three, I mentioned the meet and greet as a way to get to know your leaders. When you are meeting with them, this is a great opportunity to ask them for their preferred communication style. Do they prefer phone calls or email? Are there certain times of the day you can reach them in person, by phone, or by email? When you mirror their communication style, leaders will see you more like a business partner and less like an obstacle.

Quick Tip: Mirror Their Communication Style

Ask a Trusted Resource. Another way to identify a leader's communication preference is to ask a trusted resource, such as your supervisor.

Communicating Diplomatically with Physicians

When it comes to communicating diplomatically with physicians, many of the strategies mentioned above for communicating with healthcare leaders equally apply to physicians. With that said, communicating with physicians is a distinct enough challenge to warrant mentioning some additional approaches.

Though both audiences are highly educated, the similarities end there. First, physicians tend to be more competitive by nature. Their educational experience consisted of striving to be the top of their class in order to enhance their career path. Also, physicians, unlike healthcare leaders, were trained to be autonomous decision makers. As a consequence, physicians have an internal expectation to be efficient with their decisions. The autonomous decision-making trait of physicians is much different than the groupthink model of healthcare leaders. This decision-making approach is what often frustrates some physicians about the pace of decisions made by healthcare leaders. In a book-called *Getting It Done: Experienced Healthcare Leaders Reveal Field-Tested Strategies for*

Clinical and Financial Success,[8] Dr. Kenneth Cohn discusses collaboration between healthcare leaders and physicians. During his research for the book, Dr. Cohn interviewed MBAs and physicians about what percentage of their training was based on team projects. The MBAs stated around 30 to 50 percent. And the physicians? They said "Zero." Finally, physicians are specifically trained to be precise. As a result, they tend to expect the same from those they work with (clinical or administrative staff).

As it relates to compliance, generally speaking, getting buy-in from physicians can be a bit tricky. Since physicians are trained to make their own decisions, they tend to not like to be told what to do. Unfortunately for you as the compliance officer, they will see your communications with them as doing just that. Additionally, some physicians tend to feel "the rules" are a nuisance, getting in the way of providing patient care. So how can you shift a physician's mindset from "You can't make me do that" to one that is engaged in compliance? Below are some communication strategies that will help.

Define Your Message Going In

When you're communicating with physicians about a compliance matter, before meeting with the physician, define your message going in. More specifically, what are your concerns, and what is your rationale for those concerns? For example, assume you have identified a lack of documentation in the medical record to substantiate the billing of a particular physician service. In that case, you need to be able to articulate the specific concern, have documentation of the billing requirement at issue, and outline other regulations impacting billing for the service (e.g., the False Claims Act).

As part of defining your message, you also need to make sure you have identified any action items you are expecting from the physician. Continuing with the above example, outline what documentation must be present in the medical record going forward.

One final thought to add here is that if you're working through a complex matter, you may want to consider running the discussion past a physician leader first (such as the CMO or medical director). Since other physicians are the constituency for physician leaders, their interests will be aligned with yours to ensure that the discussion goes smoothly with the physician. For that reason, they can provide helpful and constructive feedback to help shape the eventual discussion with the physician.

Quick Tip: Define Your Message Going In

Outline the Discussion. To help define your message, draft an outline of the discussion that includes the background, specific concerns, and recommendations of specific actions needed to prevent future occurrences going forward.

"So What Do You Need from Me?"

If there is one single piece of advice I could give you related to physician communications, it is this: before you have a conversation with the physician, make sure you can answer in your head this question: "So what do you need from me?" Taking this approach is consistent with my earlier comment about making sure you have identified specific action items needed from the physician.

Early in my career, I learned this lesson a few times… the hard way. After communicating with physicians on various topics without putting thought into how the discussion might unfold, I consistently ran into this response. I got too focused on what I wanted to say in explaining a concern that I failed to be prepared for a basic question from the audience's viewpoint.

Being prepared with a response to that question will help you in your communication with the physician for a couple of reasons. First, it demonstrates being efficient with the physician's time, which they will appreciate. Second, by seeing the topic from the audience's viewpoint, it will enhance their trust in you that you understand their POV. In my experience, taking this approach has helped me in gaining buy-in from physicians to the compliance program.

> ***Quick Tip: So What Do You Need from Me?***
> **Defining your Message.** As part of outlining your discussion and defining the message, include this question and determine what your response will be.

Leverage Physician Champions

Another way to diplomatically communicate with physicians is to leverage support from any available physician champions, such as the CMO or medical director. If you work in a hospital setting, there will be a medical staff office with a range of physician champions who may be available. These particular physician administrative roles are designed to address both clinical and administrative concerns involving physicians. Any time you can have physician-to-physician discussion related to a compliance matter, your chances of buy-in will significantly improve. Physician champions can help communicate your objectives into terms a physician can relate to, and the physician can feel heard if he or she is in disagreement. Generally speaking, CMOs and medical directors will have "ensuring compliance with all federal, state, and local laws and regulations" as a requirement in their contract. To that end, your interests will be aligned.

> ***Quick Tip: Leverage Physician Champions***
>
> **Remember Physician Champions are Physicians.** When communicating with physician champions about a compliance matter involving a physician, follow the approaches mentioned above, such as defining your message going in and answering the question "So what do you need from me?"

Bonus material: For additional tips on how to effectively communicate with physicians, visit my Effective Communication with Physicians Tips sheet at: http://www.bluebirdhealthlaw.com/book-bonuses.

Pulling it All Together

Due to the nature of our role in the organization, we are in a position to influence the behavior of others on a daily basis. In order to positively influence behavior, you need to communicate your compliance message in a way that results in gaining buy-in from those in operations. In order to improve your chances at obtaining buy-in, you need to be able to deliver your message in a way that encourages people to participate instead of avoiding you. By focusing on communicating a message in a diplomatic manner, one that respects others in the organization, you will significantly increase your chances of awareness and buy-in. By following a strategy of using diplomacy to influence the behavior of others, you will be in a far better position for navigating the politics of healthcare.

Now that we have taken a look at how diplomacy can help us with influencing behavior, we'll shift gears and talk about how diplomacy can also help us when conflict arises. That will be the focus of the next chapter.

Chapter Takeaways

- Compliance officers are positioned to influence the behavior of others.
- Effectively influencing the behavior of others requires a diplomatic approach to communication.
- Diplomatic communications require skills in active listening, asserting your opinions, and exercising self-control.
- As you are communicating with leaders, always be mindful of efficiency and multiple POVs.
- Diplomatic communications with physicians require defining your message and clearly stating what is needed from the physician.

Chapter Seven

Using Diplomacy to Resolve Conflict

In the middle of difficulty, lies opportunity.
—Albert Einstein

Imagine you're the compliance officer for ABC Medical Center (ABC), a medium-sized health system with multiple facilities, including several hospitals. ABC offers bariatric surgeries as part of their surgical program. CMS has recently implemented a change related to required medical necessity documentation for Medicare patients undergoing bariatric surgery. More specifically, a new clinical assessment form must be completed before the procedure. As part of your role as compliance officer, you'll need to revise ABC's current processes, amend existing policies, and educate the appropriate staff on the new changes. Shortly after this communication, you receive emails from the directors of scheduling and the surgery department, both of which are affected by the change. They are frustrated with the level of work needed to comply with the new requirement. The director of scheduling feels it's the responsibility of the surgery department to ensure the documentation is in place. The director of surgery on the other hand thinks the scheduling department should own this work.

Despite your best efforts to influence behavior through diplomatic communications, there will be times when you are faced with no other option than to resolve conflict. Within the business of healthcare, there are routinely conflicts based on competing self-interests—conflicts among physicians, conflicts among staff, conflicts among physicians and staff, and conflicts among physicians or staff and patients. Sometimes these conflicts cross over into a compliance matter, placing you right in the middle trying to gain consensus. There are a number of reasons why conflict exists in the workplace: opposing viewpoints, competition among coworkers, power struggles, egos, pride, false assumptions, jealousy, lack of communication...or just plain ol' someone having a crappy day. Regardless of the reason, there remains a constant thread: conflicts are political. For that reason having a consistent process for resolving conflict will help you in navigating the politics of healthcare. Below is one approach that has helped me over the years.

Note: For purposes of clarity, I am presenting the below approach in sequential order; however, in practice these steps are often carried out simultaneously.

Step One: Identify Parties and Negotiation Styles

The first step to resolving conflict is to focus on two areas: identifying the parties involved and their negotiation styles. While identification of parties is self-explanatory, understanding negotiation styles requires some additional explanation. In chapters two and five, I talked a lot about getting to know your healthcare leaders. Aside from the previous reasons mentioned justifying why it is important to do this, understanding a leader's negotiation style is yet another rationale.

If you have taken the time to get to know a leader prior to the conflict at hand, you will have an advantage for understanding how they think and operate. This intel puts you in a position to more quickly identify how they will approach conflict. If you haven't worked with the individual, there are two ways you can approach this step. First, confidentially ask those you trust in your inner circle to find out how the leader negotiates conflict. Your supervisor may be your best option here. The second approach is to allow this information to naturally present itself as you work through the remaining steps of resolving conflict. This approach admittedly requires a little more patience and willingness to accept the unknown as you move forward.

When it comes to negotiation styles related to conflict, Kenneth W. Thomas and Ralph Kilmann's Conflict Mode Instrument (TKI)[9] categorizes an individual's negotiating style as falling into one of five categories:

1. Competing
2. Collaborating
3. Compromising
4. Accommodating
5. Avoiding

Under the TKI, there are two axes related to a party's negotiation style; one is for assertiveness, and the other one is for cooperativeness. Each negotiation style will then fall on a spectrum of these axes, with some styles favoring relationships over substance, as represented in Figure 7.1.

Figure 7.1. TKI Negotiation Style Spectrum

(Kenneth W. Thomas and Ralph Kilmann's Conflict Mode Instrument)

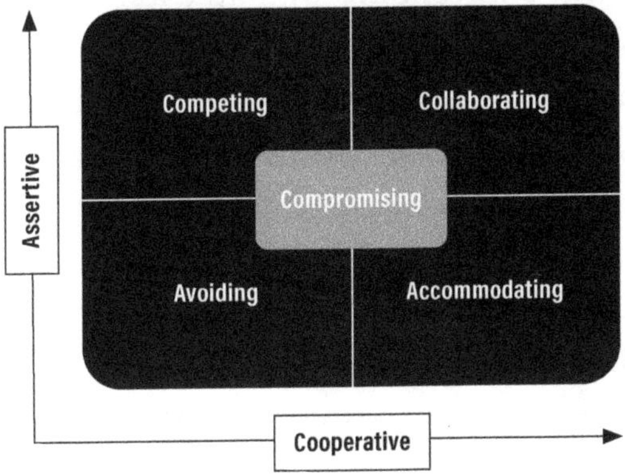

In order to understand how these negotiation styles relate to a potential conflict involving compliance and how to build consensus with each side, let's take a look at each style in more detail.

Competing ("I Win; You Lose")

TKI Negotiation Style Spectrum

(Kenneth W. Thomas and Ralph Kilmann's Conflict Mode Instrument)

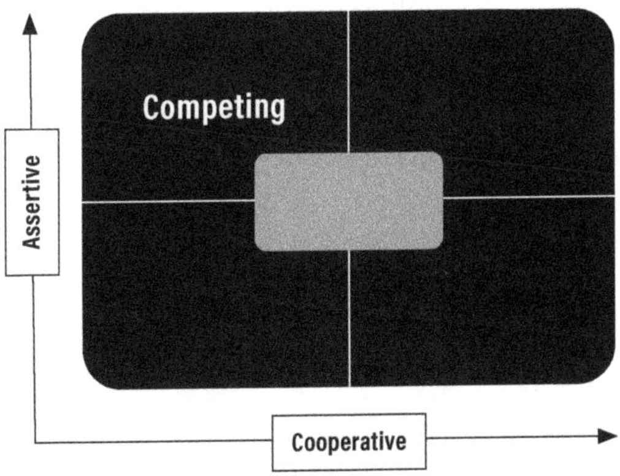

Individuals who have a competing negotiation style tend to be assertive and self-confident. A competing person's default is to pursue their own concerns with little regard to the opposing individual's concerns. A competing individual's focus is aligned more with the substance of the negotiation than the relationship. In extreme cases, a competing individual's personality can be overbearing and domineering.

Collaborating ("I Win; You Win")
TKI Negotiation Style Spectrum

(Kenneth W. Thomas and Ralph Kilmann's Conflict Mode Instrument)

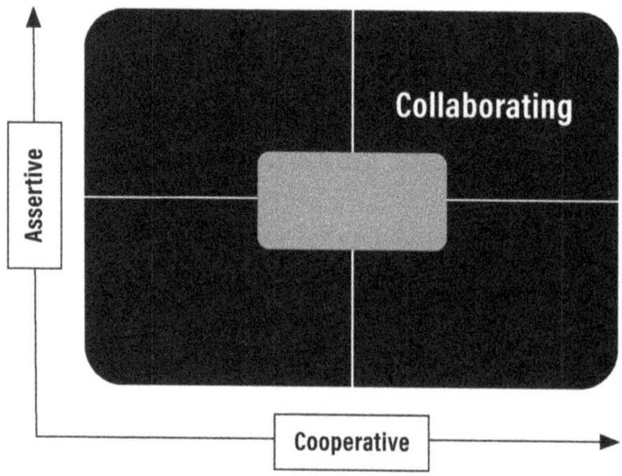

Individuals who have a collaborative negotiation style will default to cooperation by finding creative solutions that benefit all parties involved. A collaborative individual's focus is aligned both with substance and the relationship.

Compromising ("Win Some; Lose Some")
TKI Negotiation Style Spectrum

(Kenneth W. Thomas and Ralph Kilmann's Conflict Mode Instrument)

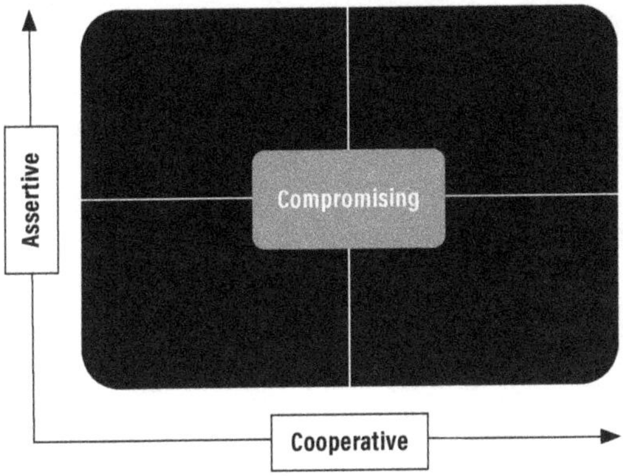

Individuals who have a compromising negotiation style tend to be assertive and cooperative. They default to finding a middle ground through an exchange of concessions by each party involved. For that reason, they are a close cousin to the collaborative style, but a compromising individual's focus is aligned slightly more with the substance of the negotiation than the relationship.

Accommodating ("You Win; I Lose")
TKI Negotiation Style Spectrum

(Kenneth W. Thomas and Ralph Kilmann's Conflict Mode Instrument)

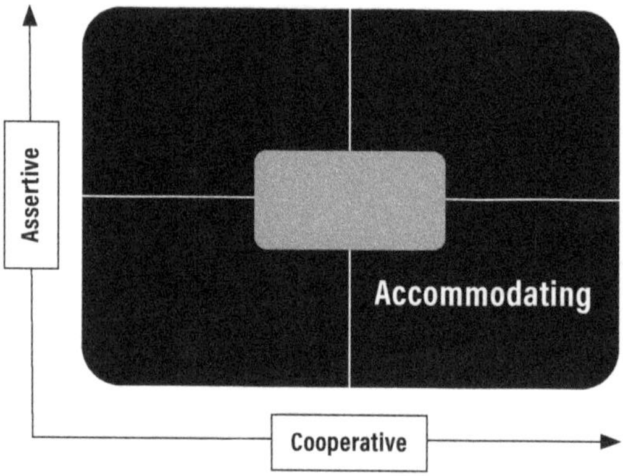

Individuals who have an accommodating negotiation style tend to be less assertive and less confident. They default to cooperating by minimizing differences and reducing tension between the parties. An accommodating individual's focus is aligned more with the relationship than the substance of the negotiation.

Avoiding ("I Lose; You Lose")
TKI Negotiation Style Spectrum

(Kenneth W. Thomas and Ralph Kilmann's Conflict Mode Instrument)

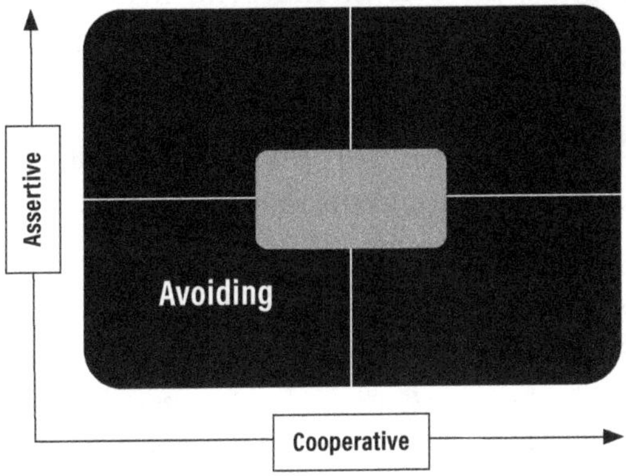

Individuals who have an avoiding negotiation style tend to be apprehensive, not assertive, and less self-confident. They default to not pursuing their own interests and creating conflict by leaving decision making to other individuals. An avoiding individual's focus is aligned more with staying neutral than the substance of the negotiation or relationship.

Step One: Wrap-Up…

Identifying the negotiation style of the parties involved in conflict can help guide you as you move forward to obtain resolution. Playing the role of independent and objective observer, focus in for a moment on the substance *and* the relationship involved in the dispute. From the viewpoint of each party, does one override the other? If this helps, Figure 7.2 includes some common traits that reside with each style.

Figure 7.2. Traits of Negotiation Styles

Competing	Collaborative	Compromising	Accommodating	Avoiding
· Self-confident · Aggressive · Assertive · Competitive · Results focused	· Self-confident · Assertive · Honest · Reasonable · Communicative · Creative minded · Solution focused · Relationship focused	· Assertive · Cooperative · Creative · Solution focused · Concession focused · Relationship focused	· Less assertive · Less confident · Less honest · Cooperative · Relationship focused	· Apprehensive · Not assertive · Less confident · Less honest · Cooperative · Neutral

When it comes to your own negotiation style, in order to effectively resolve conflict, a default position that has helped me over the years is one of collaboration. Here, you are marrying the relationship focus of the accommodating style with the assertiveness and results focus of the competitive style. Once you have identified the negotiation styles of all parties involved, the next step is to make sure you understand each party's POV related to the conflict.

Quick Tip: Identifying Parties and Negotiation Styles

Think neutral position. As you are resolving conflict, maintain a neutral position throughout the process. Once the conflict is over, you will still need to maintain relationships with all parties for the good of the compliance program.

Step Two: Understand All Points of View

While there are many different reasons for conflict, lack of information by one or both parties is often the root cause. For that reason, successfully resolving any conflict requires making sure you *fully* understand each side's POV. Understanding POV means you have identified and understand *both* a person's position and interest. Since often positions are communicated, whereas interests are not, let's take a deeper dive into the difference between the two.

A position is what a person says they want, whereas a person's interest is *the why* behind whatever it is they say they want. For example, using the bariatric surgery documentation scenario, assume I am working through this issue with the director of the surgical department…we'll call her Mary. If Mary says, "Jay, we cannot be responsible for ensuring this documentation is in place." That is Mary's position. If I were to ask Mary why, she might say, "Because I am currently down five nurses, three due to budget cuts, and two others are out on a medical leave. I am stretched so thin as it is." The fact that Mary is short staffed and feeling her staff cannot take on the additional work—is her interest. When it comes to resolving conflict, identifying interests will be the most valuable information to you in understanding a leader's POV.

While positions are often communicated publicly, identifying interests can be more challenging. A leader may not publicly disclose his or her interest, either out of concern that it is viewed as an excuse or because he or she is managing communications on a confidential topic. With that said, below are some professional approaches you can take to better understand a leader's POV, including positions and interests.

Individual Discussions

Set up a time to talk with each party offline. This can be helpful in understanding their position because you have the ability to just focus on their side of the dispute without interruption or filters from the opposing side. Having individual meetings also allows the party to feel more comfortable in speaking freely about their interests without judgment from the other side. If you have an individual discussion, just make sure the person is reassured that you will not share information without their consent if you want to maintain trust with that leader.

Empathy

Empathize with their position. In this context, I am not suggesting you agree with their position but that you demonstrate to the leader you understand their concerns and *the whys* behind them (i.e., the interest). Something I have appreciated about the healthcare industry is the fact that as industry workers, we are uniquely positioned to empathize because of the nature of our customer—the patient. Every single one of us has been a patient—or will be one—at some point in our lives. The same cannot be said for a narcoleptic who sells insomnia medication.

So how do you demonstrate empathy? One effective way is to speak back your understanding of their position and allow them to fact check you. Validating how they are feeling about a situation in conflict will also help. Here, you need to see the issue from their perspective. How would *you* feel if the same set of circumstances occurred for you? I've said this before, but it is worth repeating here, sometimes in this line of work you have to periodically stop thinking like a compliance officer and think like a healthcare leader. For example, in the context of the bariatric surgery scenario, identify how the change will each department's operations directly. To do that, you have to momentarily think like the person having to live with the rules—not as the person enforcing them.

Observation or Shadowing

Another approach to better understand a party's POV, especially when it comes to changes involving processes, is to take time out to either observe or shadow a leader's operations. This can be a beneficial approach to take for a couple of reasons. First, it demonstrates to you that you understand the logistics from the party's POV. Second, it demonstrates to the leader that you understand the logistics from their POV. If nothing else, leaders will appreciate that you took the time to try to understand their POV, which will help strengthen the business relationship. It also shows you are engaged in finding a workable solution. In my experience leaders are likely to reciprocate with engagement to the compliance program.

Advocate for Both Sides

Another way to approach understanding POV is akin to the torture all first-year law students face—that is, engaging in a mental exercise of advocating for each side of a lawsuit. After you have taken the time to meet with the leader or shadow and observe their operations, take a moment to advocate for each side. You can do this either to yourself or a trusted colleague. Pick one side and only see their side and why they are right, and the other side is wrong. Then change course and argue for the other side. Going through this thought process helps identify both side's positions and interests as well as uncover information you hadn't considered before.

Step Two: Wrap Up...

Understanding POV is one of the most critical steps to resolving conflict. It is going to be the step you spend the most time working on. It's also the reason I spent two chapters walking through healthcare leaders' POVs. Where a person is coming from—and, more importantly, why—is information you must have if you want to effectively resolve the conflict.

Quick Tip: Understanding All Points of View

Identify Positions and Interests Before You Meet. If you can, try to identify any positions and interests before meeting with the individuals involved in the conflict. This can aid in your discussion and help identify the questions you want to ask.

Step Three: Identify and Rank Negotiables and Non-Negotiables

Once you have identified the parties and negotiation styles, and you understand each side's POV, you are in a position to identify and rank each side's negotiables and non-negotiables. Put another way, what is each side willing to accept or reject? This step will require input from each side to the conflict. Depending on the circumstances and the sequencing of your work, you will see that there are a few different approaches you can take for gathering this information.

One approach is to obtain this information as part of your meeting with each side, as discussed under step two. For example, as a matter of efficiency, it may make sense to fold this discussion into understanding each party's POV. In contrast, another approach is to include this discussion in a follow-up conversation with each side after you have given each side an opportunity to explain their POV. For example, if the party has not gone through the process of verbalizing their POV, that in and of itself tends to change people's perspectives on how important their cause is to them. It may be more meaningful to let them digest their POV and schedule a separate meeting to rank what they are willing to accept or reject. Having this break in the discussion may also be beneficial for you to identify any questions you want to ask them surrounding non-negotiables.

Once you have gone through the process of identifying and ranking each side's negotiables and non-negotiables, you will be in a position to identify each side's next best alternative. The next best alternative means this: if they had to walk away without resolving the issue, what does that look like to them?

Step Three: Wrap Up…

Aside from understanding each side's POV, going through the process of identifying each side's negotiables, non-negotiables, and next best alternatives will move you closer to finding common ground. You will now have insight as to some options for what resolution may look like.

Quick Tip: Identify and Rank Negotiables and Non-Negotiables

To help identify and rank negotiables and non-negotiables, consider asking the following questions of each party in conflict:

- "What would you like to see happen?"
- "What does success look like to you?"
- "What are you willing to give up?"
- "What is the best alternative outcome if this doesn't work out the way you want?"

Step Four: Identify Common Ground to Reach Resolution

By going through the processes outlined in the above steps, you will have obtained enough information to identify common goals between the conflicting parties in order to propose a resolution. Recall back to our discussion in chapter three when I discussed some universally held POVs for healthcare leaders, such as what is in the best interest of the patient? By default, those universally held POVs may also serve as a common goal for purposes of resolving conflict.

To find common ground, there are three approaches you can take into consideration. The first is an agreement on the next best alternative. Here, you allow each side to present their side and offer their recommended alternative. Through this process, the parties mutually agree on the next best alternative. Another approach is identifying each side's strengths and weaknesses and how each side will contribute to the overall shared purpose. Finally, there is a hybrid approach. Allow each side to present their positions and alternatives, then create consensus built off a combination of each side's proposed alternatives.

Step Four: Wrap Up…

If you're going to have success at resolving conflict, you need to have an approach that includes finding common ground between the opposing parties. A key part of reaching common ground is making sure you are identifying the shared purpose or goals as well as identifying where individuals have differences of opinion.

Quick Tip: Identify Common Ground to Reach Resolution

Value for concessions. As you are working toward a resolution, strive for each side to get value for any concessions. If they are giving something up, they should be getting something in return.

Bonus material: For additional tips on how to resolve conflict, visit my Conflict Resolution Tips sheet at: http://www.bluebirdhealthlaw.com/book-bonuses.

Pulling it All Together

Building consensus requires a blend of many of the strategies we have already covered in this book such as knowing your political landscape, thinking like a healthcare leader, and building strong relationships. As you are working through conflict, remember that on each side of an issue is a person with his or her own opinions. While opinions may differ from opposing parties, each side's opinion needs to be respected. When trying to build consensus, remember that your role is to be independent and objective. Like Switzerland. Give each side the same attention and respect by understanding their positions and interests while suspending judgment. If someone is getting a little steamed, redirect to ensure the focus is on addressing the issue and not the person involved.

Now that we talked through how to use diplomacy to resolve conflict, let's move forward and talk about establishing and maintaining boundaries. That will be our focus for the next chapter.

Chapter Takeaways

- Within the business of healthcare, conflict is inevitable.
- As the compliance officer, you will periodically get pulled into conflict between other parties.
- In order to advance the compliance program's agenda, you need to develop a consistent process for resolving conflict.
- Identifying the parties and negotiation styles, understanding POV, identifying negotiables and non-negotiables, and identifying common ground can help you in resolving conflict.
- Having the ability to diplomatically resolve conflict will improve your ability to navigate the politics of healthcare.

Chapter Eight

Establishing and Maintaining Boundaries

The oldest, shortest words—"yes" and "no"—
are those which require the most thought.
—Pythagoras

Let me tell you the story of John.

John is the director of compliance for XZY Medical Center (XYZ). XYZ is a small regional independent health system. John has three employees who report to him: a compliance officer, a privacy officer, and an auditor. John's been married for ten years. He and his wife have two kids in grade school. It's December, but for the last six months, he's been consistently working twelve-hour-plus days and playing catch up for a few hours on the weekend, sometimes at the expense of spending time with his family.

John's workload first increased when the hospital's contracts administrator quit. John's supervisor offered up John to the CEO because he had experience drafting and reviewing contracts. The interim position was intended to last for two months, but the CEO still has not obtained a replacement. In addition to the interim work, John has been spending an increasing amount of time in meetings. His auditor and privacy officer are also less experienced, so he has been spending additional time responding to emails and attending meetings to help support them. A day in the life of John typically looks like this:

5:00 a.m.	Wake up and get ready for work. (He thinks about work and what he needs to get done that day).
6:00 a.m.	Leave the house for the sixty-minute commute to work. (He thinks more about work or dictates emails.)
7:00 a.m.	Check and respond to emails or meet with other healthcare leaders if it's the only available time.
8:00 a.m. to 5:00 p.m.	Attend meetings, work on various issues and projects, and juggle communications with others from meetings, phone calls, emails, texts, and instant messages. After work, he leaves at 5:00 p.m. to commute home from work. (He thinks about work and what he did not complete that day.)
6:00 p.m.	Dinner and time spent with his family (often interrupted by intermittent thoughts of unfinished work from the day).
8:00 p.m.	Put kids to bed, spend time with his wife talking about the day or watching something on TV (periodically interrupted by thoughts about work).
10:00 p.m.	Logs into work, finishing up work he didn't get to during the day.
12:00 a.m.	Go to bed.

Last week, XYZ's CEO contacted John, concerned about twenty physician contracts he has been working on that need to be finalized and signed by all parties by the end of the year. After hanging up the phone, John thinks through his other priorities before year's end, questioning where he will find the time to complete the contracts. After thinking through it, he realizes the only time he has available is in the middle of the night. He figures if he can shift his sleep schedule to go to bed when his kids do at 8:00 p.m., he can get up at 2:00 a.m. and work uninterrupted until 6:00 a.m., when he has to leave for work. His relationship with his wife has been strained for the last few months due to the increasing work demands and stress. He figures if he can work during this time, it won't disrupt the family. She's told him she is frustrated with him because he has been irritable and distant with her and the kids. She's communicated her expectation that a change has to occur to save his marriage.

Does John's workload seem manageable? Does it seem sustainable? Have you ever said yes to a new project but silently wondered when you will find the time to complete it? If John's story sounds familiar, a lack of boundaries may be an issue for you. Establishing and maintaining healthy boundaries are necessary for maintaining a work-life balance. They are also a key strategy for navigating the politics of healthcare. In this chapter we'll explore the topic of boundaries. We'll look at what they are and how to manage them. We'll also explore some common political ones that arise for compliance officers.

What Is a Boundary?

When you think of a boundary, you may be thinking of something akin to a property line between two landowners. In our personal and professional lives, a boundary is not quite so obvious. A boundary is a limit that defines you in relation to something or someone. Boundaries can be tangible in relationships, such as your workspace. They can also be intangible in relationships, such as behavior that is offensive to you. Some universal examples of boundaries include the following:

- Protecting how we spend our time
- Communicating to others about how we want to be treated
- Respecting our feelings and opinions
- Respecting others' feelings and opinions
- Maintaining personal space
- Maintaining personal privacy
- Saying no to conduct we don't want to engage in
- Saying no to work that is outside our scope of employment

The challenge with personal boundaries (as opposed to, you know, the real ones) is that except for physical space, personal boundaries don't actually exist. You have to manufacture them into existence. It's also not always clear to others where a boundary exists until after it has been crossed. As a consequence, it's not up to others to communicate when your boundaries have been crossed—it's up to you.

Why Boundaries Are Important for Navigating the Politics of Healthcare

When it comes to the navigating the politics of healthcare, boundaries are critically important assets. When clearly defined *and communicated*, they help set expectations so that everyone functions more efficiently and effectively. Boundaries also ensure you are respecting yourself by knowing when to say yes and when to say no. If you're playing offense, they help you build strong relationships with leaders, communicate diplomatically, and resolve conflict. If you're playing defense, boundaries help protect you from unreasonable encroachment from others. Whether offense or defense, establishing and maintaining boundaries allow your leaders to see you demonstrating honest communication. These actions will help you build trust, even during times when your opinion may differ from theirs.

Establishing and Maintaining Boundaries

Since boundaries are fact-specific and evolve over time, it is crucial to have a system in place for establishing and maintaining them. When you develop an approach to boundaries that is consistent in practice, it will make adapting to changing circumstances that much easier, which will help you in navigating the politics of healthcare. Below are some key steps you can take to establish and maintain your boundaries.

Step One: Self-Assessment

As with any new process change, your first step is conducting a self-assessment. Here, you will be identifying the things you consider to be boundaries. For example, do you prefer to keep your work life separate from your personal life? I know this is one of my boundaries. Whatever your boundaries are, the point of the self-assessment is to spend time reflecting on what boundaries mean to you.

Factor in Priorities and Non-Negotiables

Boundaries are derived from our values, passions, and relationships inside and outside of work. So in conducting your self-assessment, take into account your priorities in life. This will help you determine which ones you are willing to bend on and which ones are non-negotiable. As you are ranking your priorities, you need to be aware of your limits and gut feelings. Here, you want to ask yourself questions like these:

- Are there any current circumstances that are causing me stress or frustration? Why?
- Are there any current circumstances causing me unhappiness? Why?
- What boundaries at work do I need in place in order to protect my own happiness?

As you are assessing your boundaries, be respectful of your limits. You, more than anyone else, know your tolerance level in order to properly function. Be mindful of it, and identify what you need to do in order to avoid crossing that threshold. When it comes to boundaries, keep in mind that it is about honoring your needs—not judging the choices of other people.

Factor In Threats to Your Boundaries

In our professional lives, we have no shortage of individuals overstepping our boundaries on a daily basis. I like to think of these folks as "boundary burglars." These folks like to steal your time and other things sacred to who you are as a person. The boundary burglar could be a department director who sits on a response to the state for seven weeks and then reaches out to you, giving you thirty minutes to respond. It could be a healthcare leader contacting you on a Friday at 4:45 p.m. asking to produce a presentation for a 7:30 a.m. meeting on Monday morning. Oh, did I mention she's aware that you have family in town over the weekend? Or it could be an urgent (but not actually urgent) text message from an executive assistant demanding that you call her back while you're sitting in the post-anesthesia care unit with your wife and newly born child. (Not that any of these have ever happened to me.)

As long as organizations are run by humans, there will be a need to have boundaries in place. Every one of us has a boundary burglar lurking in our lives. Thus, identifying where these threats are coming from is necessary for your self-assessment.

Quick Tip: Boundaries Self-Assessment

As you are defining your boundaries, keep two questions in the back of your mind:

1) What do you want your relationship *to your work* to look like?
2) What do you want your relationships *with others* to look like?

Step Two: Put Systems in Place to Support Your Boundaries

Now that you've conducted a self-assessment and identified your boundaries, the next step is to put systems in place to support them. For example, if you have identified a boundary for time management, a system you put in place might look like this.

Time Management Boundary:

- Identifying your most productive time of the day for working on items of highest priority
- Protecting time by blocking it on your calendar
- As needed, scheduling time to work in an alternate location where you can't be distracted

Whatever the boundary is, in order to establish and maintain it, you need to have a system in place to protect it. To further illustrate how systems help establish and maintain boundaries, consider the other examples included in Figure 8.1.

Figure 8.1. Boundary Examples and Possible Systems to Support Them

Boundary	System
Meetings with productive discussions.	Require an established agenda.
Meetings that end on time.	Each agenda item has a dedicated time frame. Using a timekeeper, announce the end of the meeting five minutes before the actual end.
Focused work time.	Check and respond to email only during certain dedicated times of the day. Add an out-of-office notice indicating the times you are available to check and respond to email.
Appropriate use of "urgent" email communications.	Define for others what is considered urgent vs. not urgent.

A key consideration to any system is proactively identifying how you'll respond when a boundary burglar comes creeping in. For example, let's say one of your boundaries is protected work time, which you've communicated to your supervisor, coworkers, and direct reports (as applicable). You then get a meeting invitation during your protected time to discuss a matter that is not urgent. Will you accept the invitation and not say anything or decline and fight to protect your time boundary? Having a process in place for how you'll respond when the boundary burglar shows up will help you in not allowing your emotions get the best of you.

Quick Tip: Putting Systems in Place to Support Boundaries

Communicate with your supervisor. As you are putting systems in place to support your boundaries, be sure to communicate with your supervisor. This is especially true for boundaries related to time or work environment. This is important for two reasons: first to obtain buy-in, and second to help provide support for your boundaries.

Step Three: Communicate Your Boundaries

Boundaries are most often violated because of miscommunication—or rather, a lack of communication. Since personal boundaries don't exist like real ones, others legitimately may not be aware of when they're crossing them. For that reason, clear communication surrounding your boundaries is a necessary step. In my experience, most people appreciate clear communication because they want to know what is expected of them. With that said, communicating boundaries can be a scary thought for some people because it may feel like inviting conflict. To help overcome this feeling, yet not come across like a jerk, the key is to focus on being respectful. That means being assertive but not being aggressive.

Being Assertive but Not Aggressive

Assertiveness is a positive form of communication. You are expressing your opinion about something that you want (which is placing value in yourself), while respecting the opinions of the other people involved (which is placing value in others). Aggressiveness is a negative form of communication. When you communicate aggressively, you are offsetting that balance of value by sending a message to others that your opinion has a higher value than their opinion. Assertive communication is focused on standing up for yourself. Aggressive communication is focused on attacking others. To help distinguish between the two forms of communication, consider the following traits in Figure 8.2, and ask yourself which feels more respectful.

Figure 8.2. Assertive vs. Aggressive Communication Traits

Assertive	**Aggressive**
Tone is sincere and conversational, steady and firm. Volume is middle range.	Tone is sarcastic and inflammatory, explosive and insulting. Volume is loud.
Talking and listening.	Talking over people.
Making eye contact.	Staring at others, invading personal space, crossing arms.
Standing up for yourself.	Bullying others.
Building your self-esteem.	Damaging others' self-esteem.
Participating in the discussion.	Controlling the discussion.
Offering suggestions and proposals.	Making threats and giving ultimatums.
Recognizing your needs matter as much as others.	Thinking only your needs matter.

When it comes to communicating boundaries, an assertive approach can have several benefits. First, it shows respect for yourself, which can help build confidence and self-esteem as you are expressing your needs and wants in a positive manner. Second, it is an effective way to resolve conflict because you are placing equal value on everyone's opinions. Finally, it helps strengthen the relationship because you are demonstrating respect for others.

Quick Tip: Communicating Boundaries

Offer an alternative. If you are not feeling comfortable saying no, offer an alternative. For example, if you are asked to work on a project that is either outside the scope of your role, or you do not have any available time, you can say, "No, but [insert name] may be available to help assist." When you offer an alternative, you are still saying no but allowing them to control the course of action.

Bonus material: For additional tips on communicating boundaries, visit my Boundary Communication Tips sheet at: http://www.bluebirdhealthlaw.com/book-bonuses.

Step Four: Hold Your Ground

Once you have established boundaries, the unfortunate reality is that your work doesn't end there. If only it were that easy. Boundary burglars will always try to find a way in. And for some burglars, setting a boundary is almost an invitation to test it. Just ask a parent. The key to setting and maintaining boundaries is habits. And like any good habit, the key to creating and maintaining them—is consistency. You will do far better if you hold your ground on your boundaries by not allowing an exception in. Once you do, it will invite another…and another…and another…

When your boundary is tested, it will become your problem to address. You'll be placed at the crossroads of having to decide whether you want to make an exception or hold your ground. Now in defense of the boundary burglar, there may be times when an exception is legitimately justified. When that is the case, then you need to be clear about why the exception was made and be consistent in your approach to any future exceptions.

Quick Tip: Holding Your Ground

Exceptions and resetting. If you make an exception to your boundary due to exigent circumstances, reset the boundary once the crisis is over (e.g., "It is OK to skip the presentation with the board to take your son to his doctor's appointment. I will cover for you, but I will plan to have you follow up with the board on any requested action items…").

Step Five: Periodic Reassessment and Adjustment

Once you have established boundaries, a reality of life is that you will need to periodically reevaluate them and make adjustments. As time moves forward and circumstances change, you may have adjusted your boundaries without realizing it. For that reason it can be helpful to pause and look inward. Here, you want to focus on how you are maintaining your boundaries and whether you need to establish new ones. Some questions you can ask yourself are:

1. What have I learned about the boundaries that are being respected?
2. What have I learned about the boundaries that are not being respected?
3. What steps do I need to take to protect the ones not being respected?
4. Are there any boundaries needing adjustment?
5. Has there been a change in circumstances requiring that new boundaries be established?

Through this process, you will continue to learn a lot—first and foremost about what is important to you and how best to protect your boundaries. You'll also uncover what is working well and what is not working well. Finally, you may discover a new boundary that needs to be addressed.

Quick Tip: Periodically Reassessing Boundaries

Routine reassessment. A good habit to get into is to set a calendar reminder to routinely set aside a certain time to go through this exercise, whether it's once a month, once a quarter, or once a year.

Now that we have covered a process for establishing and maintaining boundaries, let's take a look at some of the common political boundaries you'll encounter as a compliance officer. After identifying each boundary, we'll follow-up by taking a look at how to overcome them.

The Time Boundary

Imagine it's 3:15 p.m. on a Wednesday. You're sitting in a meeting that was supposed to have ended at 3:00 p.m. You have another meeting at 4:00 p.m., and you have a time-sensitive email that your supervisor asked you to send out, which will require at least fifteen minutes to research the answer and another ten minutes to draft the response. You also just got a text from your loan officer, who is approving a loan for your new house. He says he needs some financial information before 3:30 p.m. in order to lock in your interest rate. As you're sitting in this meeting, you're trying to be polite by participating in the discussion, but your mind is clearly elsewhere. With each passing minute, you're feeling increasingly stressed.

Nothing can be more frustrating than having a meeting that runs long, putting you behind schedule. It is even worse when people hold you hostage while they gossip endlessly about non-work-related topics. Your time becomes an important boundary that you must protect.

Other threats to the time boundary are distractions. A constant bombardment of emails, phone calls, text messages, IMs, or people stopping by throughout your day to discuss something that "will just take a minute." Unless you protect this time by establishing time boundaries, you'll never get anything done.

So what can you do to protect this boundary? For starters, take the time to assess and continually reassess how your time is being managed and who is managing it. (Is it you or someone else?) That also means being open and transparent with others about your time boundary. I'm not suggesting you be a jerk about it; rather, respectfully communicate that you need to be cautious in how your time is managed. For example, when it comes to meetings, clearly communicate before the meeting begins that you have another commitment immediately following the meeting. If you are the one running the meeting, be respectful of others' time by ending the meeting on time. Another approach you can take is to set aside dedicated blocks of time when you can focus on high-priority tasks that you need to complete without distraction. Whatever steps you take to protect this important boundary, make sure you are communicating so others are aware of your time boundary.

Quick Tip: The Time Boundary

Establish meeting buffer zones. Create periodic blocks on your calendar ("buffer zones") to avoid numerous back-to-back meetings so your brain has a chance to reset itself. Whenever possible, try to limit back-to-back meetings to no more than two or three.

The Communication Boundary

Communication is another boundary that tends to get trampled on. When communication boundaries are violated, there can be a trickle-down effect, impacting your time and workspace boundaries as well. In an age of increasing communication technology, there is a corresponding increase in distractions at work. With so many different forms of communication, many of which are equally instantaneous, there can be days where you feel you got absolutely nothing accomplished but communication. There can also be days when communicating with others feels like directing traffic as you decide who has to wait to communicate with you and who gets to proceed.

So what can you do to protect this boundary? First, you want to identify your communication preferences, much like I pointed out in chapter six when I was talking about mirroring the communication styles of your healthcare leaders. Here, you want to identify which form of communication you prefer based on your circumstances. There may be times when email is a great communication tool. For example, let's assume you're discussing a complicated issue, and you may want to refer back to the email in the future. Email can also control the pace of communication as opposed to in person, an instant message, or a phone call. On the other hand, email takes time. Depending on what's being discussed, it may take forty-five minutes to type out a carefully worded email that would take five minutes to explain in person or on a call. Once you have identified which form of communication you prefer based on your circumstances, then follow through by communicating your preferences to others so that they know.

Another step you can take for email, IM, or text communication is including in your response when you are available to further reply to the message and matter. Finally, a step you can take is to limit the amount of time you spend checking and responding to email. If email is becoming too distracting, a good rule of thumb is to check it two or three times a day:

1) At the beginning of your day
2) In the middle of your day
3) At the end of your day

Truly urgent matters should be reserved for other forms of communication, such as calls, IM or texts. By taking these approaches, you'll be setting expectations and boundaries for reasonable response times to email communication.

Quick Tip: The Communication Boundary

Define urgent matters. Another way to protect your communication boundary is to establish and communicate a definition of what is an urgent matter that requires an urgent form communication, such as a text or IM.

The Operational Work Boundary

Another common boundary issue is when an operational boundary burglar tries to get you to do their work. Now if you're a people-pleaser type, you are especially vulnerable to this type of boundary issue, so pay attention. The skilled boundary burglar (the "super-delegator") can smell your vulnerability a mile away, and they will pounce on it any chance they can get.

So how do you protect this boundary? Up front, counteracting these types of boundary burglars will require assertive communication and being comfortable with saying "no." You also need to be adept at detecting when this boundary is being crossed. While that may sound simple enough, there can be times when the boundary burglar is trying to push work off onto you without you even knowing it. A common scenario in which this occurs is when a business decision needs to be made, but it gets presented as a "compliance decision."

For example, let's assume you work in a hospital setting and a call comes in from a patient-mother, alleging that a certain nurse on your labor and delivery unit was rude to her during her stay. There is no allegation of a violation of a law, regulation, or policy, it's just a customer-service related complaint. You follow up by calling your labor and delivery director to alert her and ask for assistance. She says "Oh, I remember this patient, she was the one being rude. She called me this morning while I was in a meeting." This director tells you the nurse did nothing wrong, and that you can tell the patient the matter was looked into and resolved.

I'm sorry what? You need to call her back? But you don't even have a clinical background. Yes, "other duties as assigned" is likely in your job description, but that doesn't include tasks that are outside the scope of your role as a compliance officer. So be careful about work getting presented to you as your responsibility when it falls outside the scope of your role.

> ***Quick Tip: The Operational Work Boundary***
> **Is it within the scope of the compliance program?** When these types of requests come in, first pause and take a step back to make an assessment. Is the requested task within the scope of your job description or the compliance program?

The "Legal Advice" Boundary

A close cousin to the operational work boundary is the legal advice boundary. There will be times when operational leaders come to you asking for what is actually legal advice instead of compliance advice. To be fair, it's reasonable to confuse the two because there are circumstances (e.g., an investigation) where legal and compliance do work together on an issue. Further confusing the fact is if you're a compliance officer possessing a law degree or your compliance department reports up to your legal department.

The distinction between these two groups resides in their area of focus. Compliance is focused on preventing and detecting "compliance risk" (e.g., regulatory or policy violations). Legal is focused on reducing organizational liability associated with risk, but that risk could be compliance related risk or other forms of risk, such as criminal conduct or patient safety.

Where this boundary tends to get crossed is when a healthcare leader doesn't see this distinction and comes to you expecting you to answer a question that is liability-related risk. I'll give you an example. A CEO comes to you, mentions that she just found out they never signed a contract with a physician who is providing services to the organization. She then asks you if there is a Stark law or Anti-kickback Statute (AKS) violation. While you can advise as to whether or not the conduct is meeting the regulatory requirements of Stark or AKS, a determination of whether or not the law has been violated must come from a licensed attorney.

So how do you handle this boundary? Up front, be mindful of the potential for confusion and respond with clear communication to your leaders. That means you may need to take a step back and explain the difference to your audience, and that responding to the question is outside the scope of your role as the compliance officer. Additionally, recommend they contact your legal counsel instead. This can be accomplished either by redirecting them to legal or forwarding the communication over to legal for them to respond. When you do so, be sure to include your rationale for why the question is a legal question and not a compliance question.

Quick Tip: The "Legal Advice" Boundary

Communicate early and often. This is a constant challenge to your boundary. You'll need to communicate to others when the boundary surfaces and why you're not able to cross it.

The Bending-the-Rules Boundary

Another test of boundaries are requests of the compliance officer to bend the rules to fit the organization's business agenda. In this context, I define "the rules" as laws, regulations, or internal policies and procedures. For example, consider a CEO who is wanting to provide a gift to a physician that does not fall within the scope of what is permissible under the fraud and abuse regulations. (This is similar to what I mentioned in chapter one with the electronic device gift.) The CEO is coming to you seeking permission to make an exception to the rules. Though you have previously communicated the limits of giving such a gift to a physician, the CEO is coming back again asking you to make an exception, perhaps thinking your answer will change the second time around.

So how can you overcome this boundary? Generally speaking, the first thing you need to do is make sure you have already dug into the facts and that you fully understand them. You should have made a determination that no available exception exists permitting the conduct. You also should have made an attempt to find a solution that is compliant and business friendly. Outside of taking those steps, be clear with the healthcare leader about the limits of the rules and the consequences for violating them. I have seen a lot of compliance officers not take the extra step and explain *the why,* which creates problems down the road. Either it leaves the audience still confused as to what they can and cannot do, or it causes them to go around you in the future and do what they want to do. In either event, not taking the extra step carries the potential for a little mess to become a big one. The result is more work for you in the end.

As a last resort, if you're absolutely not able to convince the leader to avoid making an inappropriate business decision, then there may be a few paths to take depending on the level of risk. For example, at a minimum, make sure you have documented what advice you have provided and what decision operations ultimately ended up making. You may also need to consider reporting the matter to your supervisor, to legal counsel, to the compliance committee, or to the board if any of these avenues seem reasonable and appropriate. If none of those issues resolve the matter, and if there is a high level of risk, then you may need to consider whether or not to report the matter to a government agency or retain legal counsel.

Quick Tip: The Bending-the-Rules Boundary

Message your role as protector. As you are communicating about this boundary, it may be helpful to form your message in such a way that you're advising the leader. Here you can point out that you are trying to help protect the individual and the organization from compliance risk associated with his or her business decision.

The Challenging-Your-Sense-of-Ethics Boundary

Another boundary closely associated with the bending-the-rules boundary is when your sense of ethics is challenged. Billing-related issues, business relationships with others, and conflicts of interest—there is no shortage of tests that will come your way for doing the right thing. There's no hard and fast rule defining what is a challenge to your sense of ethics;

it is going to be subjective to you. For me, I tend to follow the late US Supreme Court justice Potter Stewart's test for obscenity under the First Amendment: "I know it when I see it."[10] As a compliance officer, your primary role is to ensure the organization isn't getting in trouble with federal, state, and local regulations. Relatedly, that means ensuring that others in the organization are acting with integrity when it comes to making business decisions.

So how do you overcome this boundary? First and foremost, follow your gut. What is it telling you? If you're faced with a difficult decision to make, are you finding that when you revisit your decision, you're coming back to the same answer? If so, then your gut is telling you the right decision to make. What about when your gut conflicts with the opinions of those you work for? When this occurs, you lead by communicating this boundary and, similar to the bending-the-rules boundary, communicating *the why* behind it. You can also leverage the compliance program, any organizational policies, and your organization's code of conduct to help support your boundary. Unfortunately, rules are objective in nature, and ethics are subjective, and you may not be able to convince others of the right decision to make. If there is not a way to resolve the issue, then make sure you have documented your boundary and the decisions others have made to cross it. In the long term, you may need to consider some of the other paths I mentioned above under the bending-the-rules boundary or whether the organization's corporate culture is a good fit for you.

Quick Tip: The Challenging-Your-Sense-of-Ethics Boundary

Find common alignment. One way to maintain this boundary is to find common alignment, such as doing what is in the best interest of the patient or the organization.

The Work-Life-Balance Boundary

No matter where you work or whom you work for, another boundary that gets challenged is your work-life balance. Compliance work is relentless in nature. There are always new issues to address and new regulatory changes to manage. With that said, if you want to survive, keep your worlds apart between your personal life and your business life. When you're at home, you should be spending time with your family or loved ones and engaged in whatever is important to your world. Similarly, when you're at work, you should be focused on work and not your personal life. Now, that may sound like "Hah! Easier said than done Jay!"

So what steps can you take to overcome challenges to this boundary? For starters, assess your priorities in your life (e.g., family, friends, work). Be honest with yourself about where you are currently ranking these priorities. Once you do, ask yourself, "Is this the ranking I want for my life, or do I need to readjust?" Periodically check back in with this list and adjust accordingly.

Second, assess your current work-life balance to determine whether there are some changes you can make. For example, are there processes that could be automated or delegated to reduce your workload? Through this process, you may also identify systems you can put in place to help support this boundary; for example, turning off email alert notifications on your phone when you're not at work, engaging in calming activities (e.g., meditation), or other activities to put a break in between your work life and home life. I'll give you one I am working on right now. A few months ago, I took up the drums. I've found that taking a few minutes after work to focus on playing them is almost meditative and quickly takes my mind off of work, allowing me to be present at home.

Some of the other boundaries we've discussed earlier (e.g., time and communication) can also be contributing factors to work-life imbalance, so consider whether adjustments need to be made in those areas in order to support this boundary.

Finally, when it comes to work-life balance, challenge yourself to say "no." Often, a key factor in work-life imbalance is attributable to an unmanageable workload. If you're continually getting requests for work beyond what you're *reasonably* capable of, then get comfortable with saying no to others—but offer an alternative.

Quick Tip: The Work-Life-Balance Boundary

Define your purpose. If you have not already done so, part of your work-life balance assessment should be determining your purpose in life. Is your current work-life balance supporting your purpose?

Recognizing the Boundaries of Others

Throughout this chapter, I have included a great deal of the discussion on our boundaries, but successfully navigating the politics of healthcare means recognizing—and respecting—the boundaries of others. For example, consider as a starting place societal boundaries, such as avoiding conversation around taboo topics such as politics or religion. Additionally, consider many of the aforementioned boundaries we have covered, but flip the script, and apply it to others in the organization. Are you equally respecting other people's boundaries?

Quick Tip: Recognizing Other People's Boundaries

When in doubt, ask. If you are not sure about other people's boundaries, then consider asking. Position the discussion as you wanting to better serve them by understanding what boundaries they have in place.

Pulling it All Together

In our professional lives, we have no shortage of individuals overstepping our boundaries on a daily basis. Creating and maintaining boundaries is integral to the daily life of a compliance officer. Specific to the politics of healthcare, boundaries are an important asset. They build strong relationships with leaders, help us to communicate diplomatically, and effectively resolve conflict. Boundaries also help protect us from others. For these reasons, knowing how to effectively establish and maintain boundaries will help you in navigating the politics of healthcare.

Now that we have covered establishing and maintaining boundaries, we will explore some ways to maintain professionalism in your communication in order to avoid your emotions getting the best of you. That will be our focus for the next chapter.

Chapter Takeaways

- A boundary is a limit that defines you in relation to something or someone.
- A boundary can be tangible (e.g., work environment), or intangible (e.g., offensive behavior).
- Establishing and maintaining boundaries requires a consistent process that includes self-assessment, communication, holding your ground, and periodic reassessment.
- Effectively managing boundaries will help you in navigating the politics of healthcare.

Chapter Nine

Professional Communication Strategies When Tantrums Aren't an Option

A professional is one who does [his/her] best work when [he/she] feels the least like working.
—Frank Lloyd Wright

The work of a compliance officer constantly challenges your ability to remain professional. When you consider the organizational risk involved in our work, combined with the politics of healthcare, you have a recipe for frustration, stress, and anxiety. Whether you are working through a complex issue, battling defensive leaders, or playing peacekeeper between competing self-interests, there is no shortage of opportunities to throw fits akin to that of a toddler. Unfortunately, for your career longevity, it's not an option.

Professionalism is about how you conduct yourself in the workplace. It's a skill that takes most people (myself included) years to develop through experience, which means a few self-esteem workshops will be included along the way.

Over the years I have found that intrapersonal skills (your internal communication), and interpersonal skills (your external communication) can aid in your ability to remain professional. There are a number of other resources you can consult by experts on those topics, such that I felt talking about them here would be doing a disservice to you. Instead, I thought it would be more valuable to talk about some professional communication strategies that have helped me in navigating the politics of healthcare. While not an all-inclusive list, these are ones that either helped me avoid creating a mess or reducing the size of the one. My goal in sharing them with you is to help minimize the number of self-esteem workshops that you have to endure.

Balance Politeness with Honesty

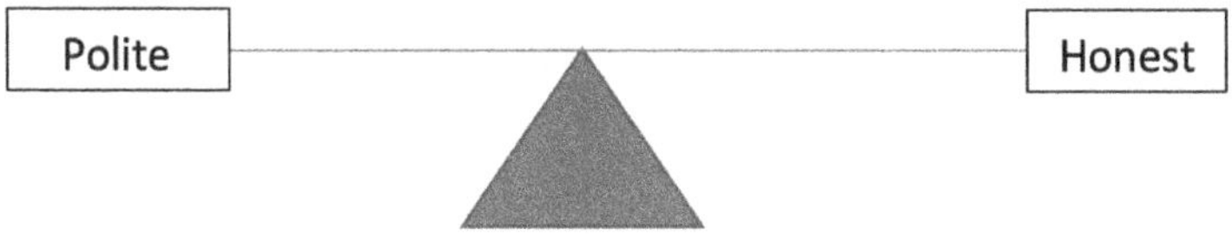

If there is a backbone to professional communication, it is communicating in a manner that is polite but honest. And it is a balancing act. If you're more honest than polite, you may be perceived as rude or insensitive. If you're more polite than honest, you may be viewed as untrustworthy or deceitful. So how do you strike that balance?

For me, I think about the balance as being guided by being respectful. Respectful communications include both elements of honesty (i.e., the content of your communication) and politeness (i.e., your approach in delivering the communication). For example, let's assume you get a new request from a healthcare leader to consult on a proposed business initiative. Let's further assume working on this request exceeds your available time when you factor in your current priorities. If you are too polite when communicating with the leader about your available time, you can overburden yourself by taking on more than you can reasonably handle. This will lead to feelings of stress because you are short on time. You may also experience feelings of regret about not being honest with the leader about the current state of your workload. On the other hand, if you say, "I don't have time for this right now," it may come off as being rude. So where is the balance? The answer can be found in having an honest discussion with the other person about your workload and competing priorities.

While it is important to tell the truth, we need to be mindful about how we carry out our messages. Balancing politeness against honesty allows you to be honest but respectful of others' feelings or opinions. When you communicate this way, you will be in a better position to preserve the relationships with your leaders and build credibility over time.

Quick Tip: Balancing Politeness with Honesty

Do you want to be liked or honest? If you are struggling with communicating honestly with others, ask yourself, "Do I want to be liked, or do I want to be honest?"

Maintain a "No Surprises Act" Communication Plan

Another component of professional communication is following what I like to think of as a "No Surprises Act" communication plan. I've mentioned a few times in this book that healthcare leaders do not like to be surprised. That is true whether one of their direct reports is notifying them of a budgeting or clinical care mistake, or if you as the compliance officer are notifying them of something like an overpayment. When it comes to communication about compliance issues, you want to avoid dropping a surprise on your leaders as much as possible. The same policy should be applied when communicating with your supervisor. Taking this approach will help you maintain a strong business relationship with both audiences.

While such a communication plan sounds like a no-brainer, the reality is that certain parts of your job will force you to strategically think through when to communicate with others in the organization. For example, if you are working on an investigation that has political implications (e.g., investigating one of your senior leaders), you may need to find a sweet spot between not alarming others unnecessarily and avoiding a surprise. In chapter ten we'll explore this topic a little more in the context of organizational communication being one of the common political battles you'll have to navigate.

Quick Tip: Maintain a No Surprises Act Communication Plan.

Put yourself in the shoes of your audience. If you're working on a compliance matter and faced with making a decision of when to tell someone what you're working on, put yourself in their shoes. Ask yourself, "If I were in this person's role, when would I want to know this information?"

Develop a Strategy for Delivering Bad News

Piggybacking off the No Surprises Act communication plan, if you are delivering a message to a healthcare leader that is filled with some unpleasant news, then you should develop a communication strategy. Let's consider an example and what a strategy might look like.

Assume you were working on resolving an identified billing and coding issue for a high dollar surgical procedure. You have conducted an investigation and determined the organization does not have documentation to substantiate medical necessity as required by CMS. In addition to addressing process changes to correct the issue going forward, you have identified a six-figure refund that must be paid back to Medicare. Given the financial impact to the organization, it is likely your leader is not going to too thrilled to hear this news. Additionally, let's assume that through the investigation, it has become clear the issue could have been prevented if the leader had held one of his or her direct reports more accountable. So you have the potential for the leader to take your news personally. How would you go about approaching your discussion with the leader?

If it were me, I would spend some time thinking about a strategy. As part of my thought process, I would make sure I have identified a communication plan around two topics:

1. How will I mentally prepare the leader to hear the news?
2. What is my recommended solution to resolve the issue and prevent a future occurrence?

The first question is really aimed at softening the blow of the news you're about to deliver. It's no surprise that as humans we tend to have a fight or flight response when confronted with shocking news. Just think about times when you found out about a catastrophic news event. The same shock factor can apply to a healthcare leader when confronted with news of a large overpayment, an employee suspected of drug diversion, or an employee committing fraud.

If you are working on an issue that has such a shock factor, then you need to prepare for that response. Think about being in that person's shoes and how you would appreciate hearing the information. For example, it may be best to allow the person to hear the information, process it, and then come back at a later time to discuss the topic. This approach can help ensure he or she is engaged in the discussion (and not distracted by the shock). It can also improve your chances of a more effective discussion about next steps.

You may also need to think about whether or not the leader will take the information defensively and if you can do anything counteract that defensiveness. For example, it may be helpful to lead the discussion with things the leader has done well before delivering the bad news. If multiple contributing factors were involved, you can also highlight those factors so the person doesn't take full ownership. Every situation will be fact-specific, but these approaches may help prepare the leader to hear the news you're about to deliver.

The second question is about thoroughly thinking through the discussion. In chapter six I mentioned some other communication strategies, such as anticipating questions, asking yourself "so what do you need from me," and bringing a solution when you bring a problem. These are all questions you can walk through for responding to this second question and developing your overall strategy for delivering bad news to your healthcare leaders.

If you plan ahead for how you are delivering bad news, it will improve your chances for success because you're taking a professional approach to an unpleasant conversation. In the short term, developing a strategy can help position you for a smoother conversation. In the long term, it will support your ability to build strong relationships with your leaders.

Quick Tip: Delivering Bad News

Consider Time, Place, and Manner. As part of your communication strategy, consider the time, place, and manner of your communication. You want to make sure your audience is engaged in the discussion and not distracted by other thoughts. You may also need to consider if the discussion is one that needs to occur in their place of work or a neutral location, as well as how to deliver the information (e.g., in person, phone call, email).

Don't Make Others Look Bad

Another form of professional communication is avoiding situations where you're going to make someone else look bad. Now, admittedly, that's a pretty vague statement, so let's break this down a little further. First, when I am talking about "someone else," I am referring to three specific audiences. The first are your coworkers, the second is your supervisor, and the third are your healthcare leaders (e.g., department directors, senior management, and board members). What do I mean by making someone else "look bad"? The answer is going to be fact-specific, but here's a good test. Ask yourself, "If I were in this person's shoes, would I feel shame, guilt, or embarrassment?" If so, then chances are you're facing a situation of someone potentially looking bad in front of others. To help illustrate what this might look like, let's walk through an example for each of these audiences.

First, your coworkers. Probably the most classic example I can think of relates to an email discussion: a coworker is communicating with you 1:1 and revealed a vulnerability. Maybe he or she forgot to follow up on a request and now you are being asked for help with interpreting the request. In this situation, don't respond by cc'ing this individual's supervisor. That's just going to come across as a form of public shaming. If the coworker wanted his or her supervisor included in the discussion, he or she would've included them in the email. Instead, try to assist the coworker, but also advise he or she reach out to the supervisor to confirm the specifics of the request.

Next up, your supervisor. Let's assume you're a compliance officer at a health system. You report up to a director, who reports up to the chief compliance officer, who is a senior vice president in the organization. You just got off the phone with a CEO of one of the hospitals that you cover. The hospital CEO tells you that she was in a meeting earlier in the day with some of the health system's executive team. This CEO goes on to explain that during the meeting, the senior vice president over risk management reported a concern involving a physician performing a surgical procedure. More specifically, the hospital CEO tells you it was determined the physician was not licensed to perform the procedure under state law. You learn that it is unknown whether services were provided to Medicare or Medicaid patients but for purpsoes of discussion, assume so. The hospital CEO concludes by telling you that the matter is being actively investigated from a risk standpoint, but to reach out if you need anything for your investigation related to licensure and billing compliance.

In this particular scenario, you have a potential opportunity for your boss and your boss's boss to look bad (be embarrassed). Why? Because you have a potentially high-risk issue that you're now aware of (e.g., patient safety, licensure and overpayment). It's been reported to you from a hospital CEO who was told the information from a senior vice president. There is potential that your boss and the chief compliance officer already know, but it is equally plausible that these individuals do not yet know. The reason for this uncertainty resides in the fact that your boss and the chief compliance officer are routinely in meetings at a higher level in the organization than you are. As a consequence, you don't completely know what your superiors know at this point in time. For that reason it is best to err on the side of caution and self-report the information to your boss. If you find out that your supervisor didn't know the information, taking this step helps prevent potential embarrassment for feeling like they were not completely up to speed on a matter on which they should have been.

Finally, we come to your healthcare leaders. Now, I do want to be careful here because there may be times when a little public shaming may be productive. Hah. For example, let's assume a healthcare leader was supposed to follow up with his staff for completing mandatory compliance training but failed to do so. You may get to a point, for accountability purposes, where it is OK to engage that leader's supervisor to correct the issue. So let's remove those types of examples from the equation and assume we have a situation involving a leader where the concern is an operational one and not a compliance one. Let's say it's a COO who comes to you vetting a new business venture. You conduct your analysis, and everything is compliant, but you don't know whether the CEO is aware of what the COO is doing.

In this example, you could inquire if the CEO is aware, or you could suggest that the COO loop in the CEO. If for some reason you don't trust the COO to notify the CEO, you could take the additional step of closing the loop with the CEO, but only if you have no other choice. Similar to the example involving your boss, taking this step helps ensure the CEO is not left feeling embarrassed for not knowing about something going on with a direct report. In this circumstance, the preferred route would be to ask the COO if the CEO is aware. You then can allow the COO the opportunity to loop in the CEO. That route will help ensure you maintain a good relationship with both parties.

Being mindful of circumstances in which someone might look bad and taking steps to prevent that from happening will help you in developing stronger business relationships. It can also help avoid creating a communication mess. Over time, having this sense will also help you in navigating the politics of healthcare.

Quick Tip: Don't Make Others Look Bad

Stand in the shoes of your audience. As you are working through any dilemmas associated with communication, ask yourself, "If I were in this person's shoes, would I want to know this information?" Most of the time, that can help guide your decision about whether to speak up.

Avoid "Us vs. Them" Communication

Another approach that has helped me professionally communicate with others in the organization is to avoid an "us vs. them" mentality. The Stones vs. the Beatles, Republicans vs.

Democrats, the Vikings vs. the Packers—all of these are examples of an *us vs. them* mentality. And some are rightly so—I mean, the Stones were, after all, the better band. All kidding aside, while *us vs. them* in the aforementioned context is part of healthy competition, when it comes to organizational communication, it can be damaging to the corporate culture.

In our world of corporate compliance, we see this play out with departments fighting over logistical processes. For example, similar to what we discussed earlier in this book, assume there is a new regulatory change, and someone has to own the responsibility of ensuring certain documentation is in place to bill out for a particular service. Some other examples include employees vs. supervisors or compliance vs. operations. The takeaway here is to be careful you are not falling into this mentality when communicating with others in the organization.

Quick Tip: Avoiding Us vs. Them Communications

Think Switzerland. Remember that as a compliance officer, your role in the organization is to remain independent and objective—a neutral party, like Switzerland.

Resist the Temptation to Communicate When You're *Feeling* Your Feelings

With compliance work, there will be moments when you get pulled into situations with others where emotions will run high and one or more people are a little steamed. Though not always the case, these situations often involve conflict between the organization's business and compliance agendas as well as some competing self-interests at play. Let's say a COO wants to pursue offering a new telemedicine service, but how the COO wants to provide the service is not meeting the current regulatory requirements. You have tried to communicate what is required, but the COO has not been willing to make the needed changes. If you find your emotions are starting to get the better of you, what can you do?

First, keep your focus on the issue and not the person. That means identifying areas of aligned interest and maintaining your attention on how best to resolve the situation for all parties involved. (*Note: This is where the approach to diplomatically resolving conflict can be helpful.*) To help keep your focus on the issue and not the person, find opportunities to validate the other person's emotions. This is where empathy and understanding POV will help. Another approach is to find a way to momentarily pause the discussion so you can refocus to a positive mindset (e.g., literally take a few deep breaths or count to ten in your head). A third option is to see if there is an opportunity to meet at a later time. This would allow you both time to feel your feelings and cool off. If you take this approach, just make sure that before you end the conversation you commit to meeting again at a certain date and time.

If the discussion is taking place in a written form (e.g., email, text, or IM), you will have the luxury of time, so use it to your advantage. Instead of firing off an email when you're steamed, go through the process of drafting your response, but walk away and work on something else. This break, even for twenty to thirty minutes, will help reset your emotional state. Then, go back and reread what you wrote to see if you are still feeling the same way. If so, you may need to repeat the process, but take a longer break. I have found that once I have gone through this process, I'll edit what I wrote to cut out the emotion from the written communication. Another option is to show your response to a coworker that you trust (in a way that doesn't jeopardize confidentiality).Your supervisor is often the best option. Having an objective sounding board can be a good reality check on whether your communication reads with unprofessional emotion.

Quick Tip: Avoiding Overly Emotional Communication

Email Yourself. If you are going through the process of drafting a response and walking away, then separately email it yourself. Don't hit reply and start typing. A cautionary tale: I once had a colleague draft a response, but then IT called to fix his computer. While closing down programs to help IT, he inadvertently sent the email not realizing what he had done!

Lead with a Mindset of "Maybe" Instead of "No!" When Consulting

In the world of a compliance officer, a sad reality is that with some exceptions, we don't get to be the hero. One of those exceptions can be consulting to healthcare leaders on new service lines or proposed business deals. When you're able to allow a healthcare leader to move forward in a manner that is both business friendly and compliant, it feels as if you drained a three pointer at the buzzer in overtime. OK, that might be a slight exaggeration, but the point is, these are moments when your leaders will celebrate you. Since these times infrequently occur due to our role as compliance officers, you should embrace them for what they are: an opportunity to demonstrate to a leader you are a business partner and not an obstacle.

When you are consulting to your healthcare leaders, the most professional way to approach this work is to lead with a mindset of "maybe" instead of "no!" when they come to you. Compliance questions are a world of gray because most regulations are intentionally written by lawyers to fit changing circumstances over time. Think about HIPAA. For those of us old enough to remember, when HIPAA was signed into law in 1996, there was barely an internet and email. Few of us had cell phones. There was no texting. No social media. No smartphones. If you wanted to coordinate a time and place to meet up with your buddies, you called each other ahead of time. If they answered, they showed up; if they didn't, well, they missed out. The point is, even though these forms of communication either didn't exist or barely existed in 1996, we still have to apply them to HIPAA in today's modern communication world.

When it comes to the language of healthcare regulations, there will be circumstances when it is clear you cannot engage in certain conduct. There may also be times where workable solutions do exist, ones that do not jeopardize compliance. Finding these workable solutions is the sweet spot you should be seeking when consulting to healthcare leaders. (*Note: This is where thinking like a healthcare leader and understanding their POV will help you*).

If you go into a discussion with a leader about a new business venture with a mindset of "No!", you're inhibiting your ability of finding a workable solution. Over time, it can have disastrous consequences for you and the compliance program. I say that because I have seen it happen with other compliance officers over the years. They become known in the organization as the person who only says "no." And then what happens? Their leaders go around them to find someone else who will work with them, or worse, they avoid the compliance officer and do what they want anyway. The end result is a mess that could've been avoided had the compliance officer not taken a standoffish position right out of the gate.

A culture of compliance takes a village with your healthcare leaders coming to you proactively. If that is the culture you want to foster, then you have to encourage them to come to you. Leading with a mindset of "Maybe" instead of "No!" does just that. It sends a message to the leader that you are keeping an open mind and willing to put in the time and effort to try and help them. Over time, this approach encourages them to come to you on the front end for advice rather than avoiding you and creating a mess on the back end. There will be times when "no" truly is the answer, but saying no should be the last word out of your mouth. Not the first.

Quick Tip: Lead with Maybe Instead of No!

Let's See What I Can Do! Embrace these opportunities as "let's-see-what-I-can-do" moments and not as "oh-just-go-away" moments. Keeping that positive thought in mind will change your perspective from "No!" to "Maybe."

Assume Neutral Intent until the Facts Establish Otherwise

Another component of professional communication is assuming neutral intent until your facts establish otherwise. This is true whether you are consulting to a healthcare leader or conducting an investigation. Neutral intent means it is unknown whether the person was acting with good or bad intent.

A common mistake I have seen new compliance officers make, sometimes even seasoned ones too, is starting from a mental place of assuming others are acting with bad intent. This typically plays out in communications (written or verbal), with the compliance officer making statements based on personal opinion instead of facts. For example, assume a compliance officer for a physician practice has identified a potential concern related to a payment being made under a contract with another practice. For discussion purposes, let's say the contract is for the use of an ultrasound machine. Rather than characterize the concern as not meeting certain regulatory requirements (e.g., fair market value under a Stark law exception or AKS safe harbor), the compliance officer labels the arrangement as "illegal". Taking such an approach has the potential to be received as inflammatory by those he or she is communicating with. A better approach is to focus on whether or not the regulatory requirements have been met.

When you assume neutral intent until the facts prove otherwise, you are maintaining a position of not judging others and not jumping to a conclusion without all the facts. Your communications also will be received with more respect, making it easier for you to ultimately advance your compliance program's agenda (i.e., ensure compliance).

Quick Tip: Assuming Neutral Intent

Leave Intent-Based Determinations to Legal. Intent-based determinations are a conclusion of law, based on a legal risk assessment. As compliance officers, our work focuses on conclusions of fact (i.e., whether the facts meet the regulatory requirements). When it comes to making intent-based determinations, defer to your legal counsel.

Outline Your Communications

With many of the strategies mentioned in this chapter, using an outline may help you in how you approach your communication. That is true whether the communication is verbal or written. If you are not familiar with outlining, it is the process of mentally mapping out, in a list format, what you want to communicate. When outlining, determine your objective for the communication. What are the one or two takeaways that you want to make sure the audience understands? At a minimum, your outline should have an introduction, the main points and subpoints you want to cover, and a conclusion. Figure 9.1 includes an example of what an outline might look like for communicating with a hospital CEO about a physician gift in the context of the Stark law's non-monetary compensation exception.

Figure 9.1. Outline Example

Introduction

- "Thank you for raising the question"
- "As I understand the facts, they are as follows..." (then insert facts as presented)
- "Below contains my thoughts related to your question."

Analysis

- State the rule—"The Stark law prohibits..."
- Talk about the Non-monetary compensation exception-what it is, why it applies, and the dollar limit
- Apply facts—"Here you are proposing to give a gift card to a physician in the amount of $50."
- Comment about the physician's current limit and if the gift exceeds the annual limit
- Comment about the fact that gift cards are not permissible under this exception, and why

Conclusion/Recommendation

- Conclude that the dollar amount is not the issue
- Conclude that the concern is that gift cards can't be given to the physician because they are a cash equivalent under Stark
- Recommend a tangible gift in the amount of $50 be given instead of a gift card

Going through the mental process of outlining is a great first step for several reasons. First, it allows you to organize your thoughts before you start the process of speaking or writing. For example, there are times when a single fact pattern is presented to you, but there are multiple questions that must be analyzed. Going through the process of outlining will help confirm that you have addressed all the questions that must be answered. Second, outlining helps improve the clarity of your communication. You are able to determine not only what you want to say, but *where* in the discussion or writing you want to say it. This helps ensure your discussion flows logically from one point to the next. Finally, outlining helps you from an efficiency standpoint. By taking the time up front to identify what you want to say, you reduce the amount of time you actually spend talking or writing. This is especially true in instances where you've spent time writing something, only to delete what you wrote because you realized it doesn't fit into the overall theme of your discussion.

Outlining is something I picked up in law school from my first-year professors, but it is a practice I have consistently used for over twenty years. I will outline when writing a formal internal memo or drafting an informal email. I use it for presentations and discussing certain topics in a meeting or phone call. There is not a day that goes by when I don't use an outline in some form for my communication with others.

Quick Tip: Outlining Your Communications

Set it Aside. If you have the available time, create your outline and then set it aside. Giving your brain a chance to reset helps you confirm whether you missed something on your first pass at the outline.

Bonus material: For additional tips on written communications, visit my Written Communication Tips sheet at: http://www.bluebirdhealthlaw.com/book-bonuses.

Pulling it All Together

Maintaining professionalism will be critical to your success as a compliance officer because you will need others in the organization to feel comfortable with you and trust you. If they don't, you will never get buy-in to your compliance program. If you focus on improving your ability to communicate professionally with others, it will position you to build stronger relationships with your healthcare leaders. Over time, this skillset will help you more effectively navigate the politics of healthcare.

Now that we have discussed some professional communication strategies, in the next chapter we will focus on identifying and overcoming some common political battles that all compliance officers face.

Chapter Takeaways

- Your ability to communicate professionally will be constantly challenged due to the nature of our role and work.
- In order to maintain your ability to be professional, you need to have some strategies rooted in respectful communication.
- Balancing politeness with honesty, avoiding surprises, not making others look bad, and resisting the temptation to communicate when you're feeling your feelings are strategies based on respectful communication.
- Leading from a mindset of "Maybe" instead of "No!" when consulting to leaders, assuming neutral intent until your facts establish otherwise, and having a strategy for delivering bad news are also based on respectful communication.
- Using these communication strategies will help support you in navigating the politics of healthcare.

Chapter Ten

Common Political Battles

The grass may look greener on the other side,
but believe me, it is just as hard to cut.
—Little Richard

I've been fortunate enough to have had the opportunity to be a compliance officer for organizations of all shapes and sizes. Some of them had numerous lines of business and over two hundred thousand employees, while some had a single line of business and only twenty employees. Though the size of the organizations differed, I found that many of the political battles were still the same. The tension may be due to competing self-interests or, more broadly, the organization's corporate culture.

Many of these battles are byproducts of two themes: miscommunication and misunderstanding. Many of the steps you can take to overcome these political battles reside in the strategies discussed earlier in this book, such as thinking like a healthcare leader or understanding the political landscape around you. For that reason, this chapter will focus on some of these battles and apply the strategies that we've already covered in this book. The discussion is not intended to be all inclusive but rather representative of situations I kept running into, no matter what organization I worked for. Also, these were situations I had to figure out how to overcome through experience, sometimes good, sometimes bad. My overall goal in sharing what I learned is to help you reduce the trial and error in order to effectively navigate the politics of healthcare.

Political Battle: Defensive Leaders

A common reality with this profession is that the job title alone casts negative imagery in the minds of certain healthcare leaders. There could be any number of reasons why a leader is defensive toward compliance, but generally speaking, if you are contacting them, chances are that they will have a defensive mindset before you even utter your first words. Even in circumstances in which you have a strong relationship with a leader, he or she may still assume that if you are contacting them, it's not good.

There are some common characteristics of a defensive leader. First, they can be argumentative and combative toward you, often questioning why you are asking them for information or asking them to perform a task. Second, they will expend endless amounts of energy trying to convince you why a compliance-related task is not obtainable, practical, or realistic. Finally, they may avoid your phone calls and emails or even avoid making eye contact with you. This is especially true when they know they owe you a response.

So what can you do? First and foremost, follow the strategies outlined in chapter five for building strong relationships with the defensive leader. This can help break down barriers so that they become more engaged with the compliance program. Also, understanding the political landscape will be helpful knowledge to have. Lurking in the background may be the rationale for why the leader is defensive toward compliance. Finally, there is self-awareness. Be mindful of the fact that leaders are generally assuming you're calling with bad news. If you're not calling with bad news, such as seeking feedback to help understand an operational process, then plan for an initial negative response, and proactively address it. Set their mind at ease up front by disclosing why you are calling: "Hey, Jim. It's Jay from compliance. Don't hang up! This is a good call."

Now if you *are* calling with bad news, don't let their defensiveness get the best of you by responding with equal amounts of defensiveness. Stay focused on the fact that the concern is addressing the issue, not the leader. Remember that your ultimate role is to keep them and the organization from getting into trouble with government agencies. For that reason, it may be helpful to communicate that message up front as part of your purpose in contacting them. In my experience, great healthcare leaders know that while they may not necessarily want to talk to you, they do value compliance when it comes to keeping them from getting into trouble.

Another source of defensiveness may reside in frustrations tied to a lack of understanding. For defensive leaders, it can be helpful to go the extra mile in explaining *the why* behind the information you are needing. Once they grasp why you're asking for certain information, they tend to drop their guard.

Finally, some leaders may just be defensive by nature, and there is nothing you can do to salvage the relationship. If that's the case, continue to stay the course of not fighting fire with fire. If they are defensive by nature and there is no chance of overcoming that, then likely they are behaving that way with others in the organization. In my experience, because of how they conduct themselves with others, eventually they are likely to move on, either voluntarily or involuntarily.

Quick Tip: Overcoming Defensive Leaders

Think like a leader, not a compliance officer. Follow the approach in chapters three and four for thinking like a healthcare leader. This can be helpful for identifying why he or she is defensive and figuring out a solution that will work.

Political Battle: Disengaged Leaders

A close companion to the defensive leader is the disengaged leader. This individual is a whole separate demographic, though. While defensive leaders are combative, they are at least engaged. Disengaged leaders, on the other hand, don't even express opinions; they're just a special kind of out of it, physically or mentally. These individuals will vary personality-wise, but some telltale signs of a disengaged leader include the following:

- Multitasking during calls or meetings ("I'm sorry; what was the question again?")
- Failing to deliver on requested action items ("I'm sorry; it fell off my radar. I must've found other less important things to do instead.")
- Skipping meetings ("For some reason it wasn't on my calendar.")
- Fringe listening ("Remind me—what happened again?")

In my experience, the best healthcare leaders I have worked with from an ability standpoint are the ones who were engaged with their staff, whether the topic was compliance or something else. How do you know that a leader is engaged? The answer is that they display genuine curiosity. If they ask questions to understand, that is being engaged. If they proactively come to you with questions or concerns, that is being engaged. Some may go so far as proposing potential compliance solutions to resolve an operational concern. I've had some leaders like that during my career and they were amazing to work with. Engaged leaders are your rock stars because they make your life easier. If only there were more of them.

The unfortunate reality is that not all healthcare leaders are engaged. For the ones who aren't, *you'll* have to work hard to move them over to engaged. So how do you do that? Generally speaking, follow the approach outlined in chapter five for building strong relationships with leaders. I would add that emphasis should be placed on trying to establish a rapport and connection with them. If you can recognize times when the disengaged leader supported the compliance program, that can help establish rapport. Additionally, dig into any reasons behind why they are disengaged. This can help determine the source and identify whether there is anything you can do to make their lives easier. Finally, leverage self-awareness. Don't overlook the fact that disengagement could be the result of the compliance department not doing a sufficient job to help the leader. For example, if the leader is not understanding a requirement, it could be that proper education was never carried out by the compliance department.

Quick Tip: Overcoming Disengaged Leaders

The more they disengage, the more you engage. Rather than reciprocating a level of disengagement, do the opposite. Take more of an active interest in them and their operations.

Political Battle: Poor Tone

Depending on where you are in your career, you may have come across the phrase "tone at the top" ("tone"). If you haven't come across tone, then let me introduce the concept to you. Tone represents the behavior of the senior leaders in your organization who are modeling what is appropriate professional and ethical conduct, which shapes the culture for the organization. In my experience, I have worked with leaders who demonstrated excellent tone, while others demonstrated very poor tone. My hope for you is that you don't have the latter—but, hey, if you do, then like me, you'll have an opportunity for professional growth. See? It's not all bad.

Since tone relates to the conduct of your leaders, it can impact the compliance program and be a political battle you have to overcome. For example, consider a senior leader who isn't supporting the compliance program by attending a mandatory training session. He or she has now put you in the super fun position of justifying to the other employees that *mandatory* means *mandatory*, regardless of position. It's a reasonable position for the other employees attending to say, "Well, gee. If the CEO doesn't have to be here, then why do I?" Ensuring your leaders are demonstrating good tone is important, and when they're not, educate them on the importance of tone and how it impacts trust in the compliance program.

So what can you do to overcome poor tone? Generally speaking, the approaches for understanding the political landscape around you, building strong relationships, and thinking like a leader will be most helpful. These will provide you with a starting point, but I caution that it will take time to change tone. In the more immediate future, conducting education about proper tone will be your quickest recourse. Here, you want to educate and reeducate your leaders on the importance of good tone as a matter of corporate culture and the effectiveness of the compliance program. In order to connect with your audience, use situational examples whenever possible to carry your message. Take the mandatory training scenario I mentioned above. Here, you want to put the leader in the POV of the employees and how *they* would feel when the leader doesn't attend mandatory training. Another approach you can take is to reinforce good tone. Whenever a leader demonstrates good tone, encourage future behavior by recognizing them. This will help increase their level of self-awareness about proper tone.

Quick Tip: Poor Tone

Leverage your good tone leaders. Leverage your good tone leaders to help you carry the message to poor tone leaders. Another option is to make reference to the good tone leader as an example of the type of behavior to demonstrate.

Political Battle: Business Agenda vs. Compliance Agenda

As discussed in chapter one, there are two primary agendas for any healthcare organization participating in a federal healthcare program. To recap, the first one is the organization's business agenda, and the second is the compliance program's agenda. The business agenda is driven by what is in the best interests of the organization from financial and reputational standpoints, while the compliance agenda is driven by ensuring the organization and the workforce remain compliant with all federal, state, and local regulations.

There will be times when both agendas are aligned. For example, if an employee has breached a patient's PHI, such an incident impacts both agendas negatively. On the business side, there is potential reputational risk, as patients tend to lose trust in organizations that can't handle their health information. If the breach is large enough, the organization is required to notify local media. A breach can also cause financial risk to the organization in the form of lost revenue as well as fines or penalties associated with a government investigation. Therefore, it is in the best interest of the organization's business agenda to diligently address the issue. For compliance departments that oversee privacy investigations, it would also be in the best interest of the department's agenda to respond to the matter. With any PHI incident, there is the potential for a government investigation to be triggered. If that happens, the government's focus is going to be not only determining what happened, but also how the organization responded from an investigation and resolution standpoint. To that end, both agendas are aligned to ensure the organization responds appropriately.

There also may be times when the organization's business agenda conflicts with the compliance agenda. For example, let's say you work for ABC organization (ABC), who is seeking to do business with another healthcare provider, XYZ, P.C. (XYZ). The proposal is for XYZ offer a new physician service to ABC's patients. In this scenario ABC is in a position to potentially increase revenue and its reputation in the community. That would advance ABC's business agenda. If, however, XYZ is promising to inappropriately compensate ABC for Medicare or Medicaid referrals, that creates potential fraud and abuse concerns. That conduct would not support the ABC compliance program's agenda. If ABC's leadership just wants to do the deal and not muddy the waters by addressing the potential concerns, these two agendas are not going to be aligned. When that happens, a political battle now comes into play. ABC's compliance officer must find a way to align the agendas in order to move everyone forward. The best way to do that is to make sure he or she fully understands the details and history of the potential arrangement as well as any politics surrounding all parties involved.

So what can you do to overcome this political battle? First, following the strategies for understanding the political landscape, thinking like a healthcare leader, and building strong relationships will again be your starting points. If you have gained the leader's respect, this will help you when the time comes to negotiate a deal that aligns both agendas. You can also leverage your diplomacy skills for influencing behavior and resolving conflict. These skills are critical to reaching consensus with a result that supports both of the organization's agendas.

Quick Tip: Overcoming Business Agenda vs. Compliance Agenda

Treat your role as a business partner, not an obstacle. The best way to overcome this battle is to treat your role as a business partner and not an obstacle. That means striving to find solutions that will support both agendas instead of pointing out deficiencies with no recommended alternatives to maintain compliance.

Political Battle: Finding Out after the Fact

Another common political battle is finding out about a compliance issue after the fact. This type of situation is often the byproduct of some of the earlier political battles mentioned (e.g., defensive or disengaged leaders). My personal favorite is when you're sitting in a meeting, and without warning, someone blurts out a project he or she is working on with an obvious compliance concern. Here, I'm taking the liberty of saying it's obvious because everyone else in the room—except this person, either looks concerned or is looking directly at you. Typically, this plays out because the leader wasn't entirely aware of the concern. In this leader's defense, it may not necessarily be his or her fault for not knowing. If there were others involved, though, who did know better, then someone should've taken action to help this leader. They could either advise this leader to contact you directly or to take the lead and contact you themselves. Nonetheless, once the leader begins speaking about the facts of the concern in your presence, you're now at the crossroads of a political decision to make: do you publicly address this matter in the meeting or privately offline?

Of course the typical lawyerly answer of "It depends" applies, due to your facts and circumstances. Also, there are certain advantages and disadvantages that may need to be weighed. For example, if the matter is clearly a compliance issue, it is best to address it in the meeting with action items identified to resolve it. On the other hand, if fact-gathering and research are needed to make a determination, it may be best to address it offline, so you don't unnecessarily alarm others.

So what can you do about these moments that are real and fun, but not real fun? Play the long game by following the approach of building strong relationships with your leaders. Over time, this will result in increasing their awareness to proactively engage you to ensure there are no compliance issues. As your relationships strengthen with them, leaders will feel more comfortable coming to you. Additionally, educate early and often about the need to engage compliance. Part of your ongoing compliance message to leaders needs to be emphasizing the importance of reporting concerns to you proactively instead of reactively. As you are communicating your message, provide hypothetical examples that outline how little problems can snowball into big ones. Highlight how an issue could negatively impact them if not addressed (e.g., loss of trust and reputation, potential corrective action, financial impact to organization).

For a short-term strategy, I would run through the self-control test I covered in chapter six when discussing diplomatic communication:

1. Does this need to be said?
2. Does this need to be said by me?
3. Does this need to be said now?

This list can help you in determining whether or not addressing the issue in the meeting or offline is the most appropriate course of action to take.

Quick Tip: Finding Out after the Fact

Focus on the present and future. Since you can't undo what's been done, do not focus on the past. Instead, focus on the present and future for correcting the issue. The government recognizes regulatory violations are going to occur and compliance officers can't be everywhere at all times. That said, once an issue is identified, the government does expect the organization to address them and take steps to prevent future occurrences.

Political Battle: Leader Pushback When Asking Questions

Another political battle you will encounter is when leaders push back when you are asking detailed questions. Often, this response arises as part of consulting on a business proposal or conducting an investigation or audit. Additionally, this pushback sometimes goes hand-in-hand with some of the other battles mentioned (e.g., tone at the top or defensive or disengaged leaders). Depending on how the situation plays out, once you start asking questions about a leader's operations, he or she may receive your questions as being judgmental rather than fact finding to resolve the issue. While this type of response is understandable in the context of an investigation or audit, it's the consulting scenario that leaves you sometimes baffled. You're kind of left thinking, "Now look…you came to me for advice, do you want my help or not?"

When I was in law school, my criminal law professor used to tell us that all legal analysis boils down to four words: "Is this a that?"[11] While our work is not the practice of law, I think the concept equally applies to analyzing any compliance question. You need two pieces of information, your "this" (which is the facts and circumstances) and your "that" (which is the relevant law, regulation, or other guidance).

Understanding the facts requires asking questions—sometimes very detailed questions. When leaders are reluctant to provide answers, it may be because they perceive your questions as judgmental. So be mindful of how you are asking questions. For example, if you are asking a leading question ("Isn't it true that..."), it's going to feel like you're cross-examining them. Understandably, they're going to feel the need to defend themselves. Using inflammatory language (e.g., "you're breaking the law") will also yield the same reaction. Aside from being mindful of how you are asking a question, you can also let them know your reason behind the question is to help them. Here, you proactively communicate that your rationale is understand the facts—not to judge them.

You need to be comfortable asking questions, even if the questions seem basic or make it appear as if you don't know something. In this profession, there is an unwritten expectation that new compliance officers hold themselves to thinking they have to be the expert in all things operational. I know I was guilty of this when I started. I felt like I had to know everything, and I did not want others to think I did not know how the operations worked. After I began working with very skilled attorneys, I noticed they had no concerns in stating they did not know the operational side. From those experiences I started to realize that my role was not to be the expert in operations—that is the leader's role. My role is to analyze a set of facts against the regulations. Eventually, I learned that in order to avoid feeling self-conscious about asking questions, I needed to frame my questioning so that I was asking for the leader's help.

As you are developing your questioning style, follow the approach of thinking like the leader. This will help ensure that your questions factor into how they are going to be perceived by your audience.

Quick Tip: Leadership Pushback to Questions

Develop comfort zone questioning. Below are some comfortable ways to approach gathering information from a healthcare leader and not feeling like a complete idiot:

- "I am not familiar with _____ ; please help me understand what you mean when you say _____ ."
- "_____ is an area outside of my expertise; can you tell me what _____ means?"
- "To make sure we are on the same page, can you explain ____ to me like you would to someone off the street?"
- "I am dipping my toes into uncharted waters, so please help me understand what _____ means."

Political Battle: Organizational Communication

Depending upon the size and matrix of an organization, navigating through communication with others can present a number of logistical challenges that can lead to a political battle. For example, if the people who were supposed to be "in the know" were not included in a discussion, then misunderstandings, hurt feelings, and errors can result because of the miscommunication. While there is an endless list miscommunication scenarios that can play out for a compliance officer, let's take a look at two of the most common ones I've seen that create political battles:

Determining Who to Tell and When to Tell

Almost on a daily basis, you will be confronted with two questions in your mind as you approach your work ("Who do I need to tell?" and "When do I need to tell them?"). For some issues, those questions will be pretty straightforward to answer. For others, it may be a bit more complicated. For example, if an issue involves processes covering more than one department, it may require figuring out which healthcare leaders to include. Additionally, depending on the level of compliance risk involved, you may also need to first communicate to your supervisor and any leaders over the impacted departments. From there, involve others on a need-to-know basis. Another complication is that you may not be in a position of having all the facts at the time you become aware of the issue. The question then becomes this: Do you say something now or wait until you have more information?

To answer that question, your first thought should be to have a conversation with your most trusted resource—your supervisor. I have found that going through the motion of speaking out loud with a supervisor about your thought processes can help determine the most appropriate communication plan. Having this conversation will also help you understand what is expected of you with future communications. Finally, if you sense there may be a delay in finding out an answer to resolve an issue, it may be best to proactively communicate with others identified as "need to know." During this initial communication, you'll cover the fact that the issue surfaced and what steps you are taking to resolve it. From there, continue to communicate with this group until the issue is resolved.

Failing to Close a Communication Loop

Another common communication challenge is when someone fails to follow through and close the communication loop. This is a variation on figuring out whom to tell and when to tell, but this version occurs on the back end of the issue after it's been resolved.

One way to approach this scenario is to be clear with your audience. If follow-through communication is required, identify who is responsible for further communicating with the particular audience. Another approach is to request being copied on that communication or that you be provided with documentation establishing that the communication loop was closed.

When it comes to overcoming this political battle, there are a couple of universal thoughts to keep in mind. First, whenever you are working on a compliance matter, develop a communication plan. Identify who you want to communicate with and when you plan to communicate with them. Second, always be aware of your political landscape. Often the landscape will help guide your communication plan. Finally, remember to think like a healthcare leader when communicating with them. This will help you in determining, from your audience's perspective, when they would like to be looped into certain communications.

> ***Quick Tip: Organizational Communication***
>
> **Follow a No Surprises Act Communication Plan.** Discussed in chapter nine related to professional communication, it's a good approach overall when determining any communication plan for any matter you're working on.

Political Battle: Staying in Your Lane

Another common political battle that arises is making sure you are staying within the scope of your role as compliance officer in the organization. On the surface that may seem like an obvious statement to make, but there are a couple of scenarios that can sneak up on you. If you're not careful, you can find yourself inadvertently veering outside the scope of your role. When that happens, you're on the precipice of a political battle with others in the organization. Let's take a look at each of these scenarios and how to overcome them.

When You're Asked to Go outside Your Lane

The first scenario is when a healthcare leader comes to you asking you to perform a duty that is outside the scope of your role as compliance officer. Often this occurs because the leader isn't keenly aware of underlying concerns enough to know what is a compliance issue as opposed to an issue that must be managed by another department. This happens a lot with legal or risk management. If your organization has a risk management department tasked with responding to patient care complaints or addressing clinical quality-of-care issues, those are duties outside your role as compliance officer. Those must be handled by a risk management department. When these situations occur, you need to educate the leader about what questions are within your lane and what questions fall within someone else's lane.

When You Need to Stop Yourself from Going Outside Your Lane
Another common scenario related to staying within your lane involves your own conduct. This involves a similar set of facts as the previous situation, but instead of it being the healthcare leader who needs to be redirected, *it's you* that needs to be redirected. What I mean by that is there can be times when you dive in and start working on an issue not realizing the question that needs to be answered is not a compliance question. In your defense, you may get caught up in trying to help a leader and simply overlook the fact that the question really is one for another department to address. Since you have already proceeded down this path, the best course of action to take is to first apologize—in this case, to the leader you are communicating with and to the appropriate owner of the work needed. If you have a solid working relationship with these individuals and your veering into another lane was not intentional, everyone should be cool to move forward in addressing the issue at hand.

Regardless of which scenario you fall into, there are some general approaches you can take to overcome this battle. First, educate others about lanes early and often. Since operational leaders often confuse the compliance role with other roles in the organization, educate them on which subject matters you cover and which ones are covered by someone else. Second, build strong relationships with the other departments that compliance gets confused with. This will help in times you need to partner on projects and redirect leaders to one another. Finally, when a lane has been crossed over, clearly communicate that this has occurred and redirect to the appropriate resource.

Quick Tip: Staying in Your Lane

Communicate early and often with those in the other lanes. Make sure you are continually communicating with the individuals in the other lanes that you know what subject matter is within your lane and what subject matter is within theirs. This can aid in building trust with them for any times you may have accidentally crossed into another lane.

Political Battle: Challenging Your Ethics and Integrity

Finally, your ethics and integrity may be challenged, which can become a significant political battle. For example, you may have leaders challenging you to look the other way on a legitimate compliance issue or trying to persuade you to minimize the significance of a concern. These instances can surface in the context of a competitor who is ignoring the rules—sort of the grown-up version of peer pressure ("C'mon, man, everyone is doing it…"). While having your ethics and integrity challenged is not something you'd prefer to experience, there is a positive angle. In the present moment, when these situations occur, you will learn how important integrity is to you. After the fact, you will come to appreciate how much you grew from the experience. You can also leverage the experience during a training session on the importance of speaking up when something doesn't feel right. If you can give a non-descript example of a time *you* were put in an awkward position of having to speak up—wow, talk about a powerful opportunity to connect with your audience!

In the foreground to these situations is the task at hand: What should you do with this information? How do you resolve this issue and prevent a future occurrence? In the background of these situations are the realities of your personal life testing your sense of ethics and integrity. What will happen if you hold your ground? Will you lose your job for speaking up? How will you pay your bills or put food on the table if you do lose your job? Doing the right thing sounds like an easy thing to do on paper; however, when you factor in your personal life, you find out the decision is weighted heavily by some very real consequences.

Over the course of my career, I have had incidents when my own sense of ethics and integrity were challenged. When my job was not on the line, these were easy decisions to make. There was one time, though, when I faced a decision of risking the loss of my job for speaking up about what I thought was the right thing to do. The situation related to a needed investigation involving an executive, who was also my supervisor at the time. There were several allegations of noncompliance and unethical behavior coming to me from front-line staff. At the time, the organization didn't have a compliance program yet—no code of conduct, no compliance policies, and certainly no nonretaliation policies. I was hired to put those things in place and the allegations arose just a few weeks after I started. All of the challenging questions I mentioned above are ones I had to face head-on. And it was not easy. There were times I wondered whether that day would be my last one. There were days I was completely overrun with stress thinking about the financial impact of losing my job. And there were days I asked myself, "Was doing the right thing really worth it?" So I know it is a difficult position to be in.

In this situation, I did stick with what I felt was the right thing to do. That meant moving forward with the investigation, though the supervisor could have fired me at any point. I felt like if I got fired for doing the right thing, then I could live with that. What I couldn't live with was not standing up for the employees who were brave enough to speak up to me. Since they did what compliance officers expect of them, I felt I owed it to them to do what was expected of me. Eventually, I was able to obtain support from the board to conduct the investigation, which significantly reduced the stress of losing my job. The takeaway here if you're faced with this unfortunate situation, seek out those in a position to support you in doing what you were hired to do.

When it comes to overcoming challenges to your ethics and integrity, you can leverage many of the approaches provided for you in this book. For example, building strong relationships with leaders can better position you to reduce instances of your ethics and integrity being challenged. It can also help identify allies to support you. Additionally, the approaches for diplomatic communications, professionalism, and maintaining boundaries can also be useful for effectively communicating with others.

Quick Tip: Challenges to Your Ethics and Integrity

Understanding your political landscape. When you are faced with challenges to your ethics and integrity, know the political landscape around you. This is helpful to know where certain pressures are coming from and who potentially may be an ally to you in the organization to offer support.

Pulling it All Together

The politics of healthcare will be a part of your daily life as a compliance officer. The political battles I mentioned above are ones I have encountered throughout my career. These battles are also ones I've heard numerous other compliance officers comment on over the years. In my experience, I have found them to exist regardless of an organization's size. While these challenges are ever-present, they are not insurmountable. I have come to find that the strategies outlined in this book helped me overcome these battles and effectively navigate the politics of healthcare.

Now that we have discussed some of the common political battles that compliance officers face, our discussion will shift to some final thoughts and insights about our work that I wish I knew when I started. That will be the focus of our last chapter.

Chapter Takeaways

- No matter where you work in healthcare, or who you work with, you will run into common political battles with others in the organization.
- Strategies such as understanding your political landscape, thinking like a healthcare leader, and building strong relationships will help you overcome many of these challenges.
- When you're able to overcome these common political battles, you are better equipped to navigate the politics of healthcare.

Chapter Eleven

If I Only Knew Then What I Know Now

It is good to have an end to journey toward,
but it is the journey that matters in the end.
—Ursula K. Le Guin

Now that we have talked through the politics of healthcare and discussed some key strategies to maintain a neutral position in the organization, I want to conclude with some final thoughts. Below are a few insights I have learned about myself, the compliance officer profession, and the business of healthcare. These are thoughts that I was not aware of when I started out, but looking back, now wish I had known about them. My hope is that sharing them with you will help you in successfully navigating the politics of healthcare.

You Are Always Learning

If you are the eternal student type, this job is for you. Something I learned about myself in college is that I absolutely love reading and writing. I also love education in general. When I was in law school, I knew I wanted to do something with healthcare and law. What I didn't know at the time, though, was that I would end up in healthcare compliance.

What I also didn't know back then is that compliance work provides endless opportunities for learning. Whether you are consulting to leaders, conducting investigations, or performing audits, you realize that the very nature of this profession is set up for continual learning. You not only learn about the regulations, but as you address compliance-related questions, you also learn about the organization's operations. The opportunities for learning excited me and always kept me engaged in this work over the years.

When it comes to learning about the operations, the good news is that you will learn a lot about the people you work with. The bad news is that you will learn a lot about the people you work with! Through the resolution of identified compliance matters, you will get to know the organization, which means finding out about the good, the bad—and, yes, sometimes, the ugly—that goes on in the organization.

While the good and bad can be resolved without too much agony, the ugly will challenge your ability to stay positive. When that happens, it has the potential to affect your relationships with others and your ability to navigate the politics of healthcare. In times like these, I have found it helpful to force myself to pause and reflect. I will think about the work I'm about to engage in, not about resolving the issue. A thought that has always helped energize me during this reflection period is the fact that if nothing else, I will learn something through this experience. Once I reset myself to that positive line of thought, I'm able to get back on the road again.

You Need Issues to Be Employed

Something I have learned about this profession that I didn't realize when I started out was that as a compliance officer,

I needed issues in order to have a job. Similar to the odd reality that hospitals and physicians need the sick and injured to remain in business, compliance officers need issues to resolve in order to remain employed. So if you like the mental challenge of solving problems, this profession is for you.

In my experience, I have found there is never a shortage of issues to be resolved. There will be times when you find yourself struggling to stay positive, which can impact your ability to navigate the politics of healthcare. When you find yourself struggling to stay positive, keep this thought in mind: "If there were no issues to resolve, there would be no need for me in the organization."

I can't exactly pinpoint when that thought first came to me, but I do recall the organization I was working for. I was working on a really complex issue that involved a contractual relationship with another provider that needed to be unwound. Multiple department leaders were involved, each frustrated with the length of time it was taking to resolve. There were many days I found myself struggling to stay positive, due to my own frustrations in trying to find a solution that would work for everyone. I remember thinking, "Why could they not have done it right way to begin with?" And then it hit me. If they had done it the right way, then I wouldn't be here. That thought kept me grounded, and I started to turn my negative attitude around. Eventually we got the issue resolved and moved forward. Though I left that organization a few years later, the thought has never left me. I cannot tell you how many times it has picked me up over the years and carried me to a finish line.

Measurable Growth Comes from Experiences Outside Your Comfort Zone

Over the years I have found the moments I spent working on complex issues to also be the ones I grew the most from professionally. Like that of the clinicians we advise, our profession, too, is a practice. As with any practice, your expertise is developed from functioning under repetition and uncertainty. The difference is that measurable growth comes from working through uncertain and challenging times, not from repetition.

Think about conducting new hire training on your compliance program. Once the presentation is created and delivered a few times, there is generally not a lot of variation. Over time, this information becomes repetitive and therefore offers fewer and fewer opportunities for measurable growth. In contrast, responding to your first government investigation or audit, while uncertain and probably a little scary, offers a new opportunity for measurable growth.

Navigating the politics of healthcare will provide lots of opportunities for measurable growth. Whether it is resolving conflict, keeping the business and compliance agendas in alignment, or building a strong relationship with a defensive leader, these will be *your* growth moments. There can be a tendency to see only the negatives about our circumstances when we're outside our comfort zones. Overcome the negativity by recognizing these situations for what they are—opportunities for personal growth. So embrace the times when you're outside your comfort zone. The costs are short lived, but the benefits will last a lifetime.

Building Strong Relationships with Leaders Requires a "Big Picture" Approach

Something I have picked up over the years is that the way a compliance officer interprets the initial report of a concern says a lot about how he or she will solve the problem. What I mean by that is that very quickly, you will find out whether the person is guided by the big picture or whether they're detail oriented. In order to navigate the politics of healthcare successfully, you'll be better positioned if you approach the problem as a big picture thinker. That does not mean details are not important. It's just a matter of timing. That means knowing when to focus on the big picture and when to focus on the details. In my experience those guided by the big picture do a better job of maintaining that balance. They also do a better job of maintaining a calming presence when they are interacting with their leaders. Those guided by the details tend to get so focused on the present that they can't see the future, which can create unnecessary anxiety and frustration coming from their organization's leaders.

Healthcare leaders as a group are predominantly big picture thinkers. That is because they operate in a world of mission and vision statements, strategic plans, and business agendas, all of which are focused on the big picture. That means a leader is not only focusing on the launch of a project but what the exit strategy is going to be if it doesn't work out. Big picture thinking means you're able to see what is in the past, the present, and the future.

The same line of thinking should apply to your work in furthering the compliance agenda. For example, if you are investigating an issue, what does the end of the investigation look like before you get started? If the allegation is substantiated, how will that affect you, your supervisor, and the compliance program? What impact will it have on the organization and any of the individuals involved?

Having a big picture perspective identifies what is most important, which helps you determine what is a true priority. As I said earlier, details are important; it's just a matter of timing. When a compliance matter gets presented to you for resolution, your initial interactions should be focused on the big picture. What questions do you need to resolve? How are you going to resolve them (if this is possible to predict)? Who do you need to talk to in order to resolve? What are the likely end scenarios going to be? That's a big picture line of thinking.

Over time, your professional judgment is going to be shaped by how well you can maintain a big picture view while carrying out detail-oriented work. If your goal is building strong relationships with leaders, adopting a big picture mindset will help you achieve that goal and ultimately improve your ability to navigate the politics of healthcare.

Be Adaptable

In healthcare, there will constantly be times when you are faced with competing deadlines and put in a position to have to drop everything in order to respond to an unexpected issue. When you work in an industry that functions 24/7/365, it's a given. As these circumstances arise, your ability to adapt and quickly change course will be tested. Make sure you have the necessary skills to prioritize what is most important to focus on.

When any challenge presents itself, you have a choice to make. One option is to view the situation negatively and complain about it. While it may make you feel better in the moment, this option isn't helpful for producing results in the long run. The second option is to view the challenge positively as an opportunity for measurable growth in your career. Choosing this option starts you down the path to overcome the challenge. From there, you can begin to focus on brainstorming possible solutions.

There are several benefits to being adaptable from your employer's perspective. First, it demonstrates you are an employee able to successfully manage change, making you better suited for longevity with the organization. Second, being adaptable also means being more productive. As new challenges present themselves, you are better positioned to take them on instead of expending time and energy worrying about how to get started. Finally, having the ability to adapt to change unexpectedly demonstrates the ability to lead and be resourceful.

Choose Your Words Wisely

When I was in law school, I had a professor who used to tell us, "Students, your craft will be defined by two things: your time and your words. Choose them both wisely."[12] While our profession is not the practice of law, I think the message equally applies to our work.

Something I didn't realize when I started my career is that time is your enemy. Whether you are meeting a deadline, working on a project, or conducting research, your time will constantly be challenged. There will be days of back-to-back meetings, multiple fires to put out, and urgent emails to respond to. And then the bank calls you to tell you someone has stolen your identity.

If only you had the power to hit the pause button of time, right? So far that wish has never been granted for me, though I do keep asking. Outside of some sort of supernatural power, the only way to truly battle this formidable foe is to arm yourself with skills in prioritization, time management, and honest communication. Developing these skills will be a work in progress throughout your entire career. You will continually have to make adjustments as your workload and responsibilities change.

A piece of advice related to time is this: be careful how you let others spend it. If you let them, they will allow meetings to run long, inefficiently communicate with you, or ask you to do work within their job role. Each of these circumstances will test your time boundary, which can impact your ability to navigate the politics of healthcare.

As it relates to choosing your words wisely, as a compliance officer, you will ~~play with(?)~~ ~~mess around with(?)~~ tinker(!) with words constantly in this profession. Whether you are investigating a concern, advising your leaders, or creating educational materials, the words you choose are important because they reflect the quality of your thoughts and ideas. In this book I have talked about things like assuming neutral intent until your facts prove otherwise and labeling conduct you're investigating as a "potential violation". These are just a couple of examples of being careful in the words you use when working on a compliance matter.

As you think about choosing your words wisely, let me leave you with a thought to keep in mind. Whether you are dealing with verbal or written communication, identify your audience, which means identifying any secondary audience. Once you say or write something, you never know who your communication will get passed along to.

You Have to Unconditionally Love the Struggle

I will be the first one to admit that this job is not for everyone. You *really* have to have a love for this type of work, which means an unconditional love for the *struggle* that goes along with the work. Personally, I think this true in life, no matter what you seek to do. As I've mentioned earlier in the book, I absolutely love to ski. If you were to ask my wife, she would say that I probably love it more than life itself. It's my happy place. It's where I feel like a kid again, out on an adventure. It's where I feel the most alive.

Inherent to that love, though, is an unconditional love for the struggle that goes along with skiing. Skiing means being outside in the cold, so you have to be OK with that. Being outside in the cold also means you're going to have a runny nose. Are you OK with that? And skiing means shoving your feet into ski boots. Now as much as I love to ski, I will be the first to admit that ski boots are not exactly comfortable. They're also an awkward pain in the a** to walk around in. These are all examples of the struggles that go along with skiing. These are also things I don't think about because I don't think of them as struggles. I appreciate them for what they represent to me: the opportunity to ski.

Compliance work is very similar. Deep down, you have to have an unconditional love for struggle that is part of the job, or you'll never make it. If you can happily sift through endless pages of a final rule published in the *Federal Register*, you have an unconditional love for the struggle of compliance work. That means you can see past the fact that the content is dry and the font is mind-numbingly minuscule. If a new investigation is exciting to you because it seems like an interesting adventure, you have an unconditional love for the struggle of compliance work. That means the tedious steps needed to document your work doesn't bother you. If resolving a complex issue seems like an opportunity to learn and grow, then you have an unconditional love for the struggle of compliance work. That means you're at peace with the amount of time and work it will take to resolve the matter.

In my experience, an unconditional love for the struggle is something that must occur naturally. It can't be forced. With that said, figuring out whether you have an unconditional love for the struggle of compliance work can only be identified over time. So how do you know? The litmus test I've used professionally is money. If there were no such things as money and bills to pay, would you still perform this job? Put another way, if you won the lottery tomorrow, would you still want to do this work? Going through this exercise will always provide you with your answer.

Identify What Inspires You; Consult It during Challenging Times

What inspires you? Answering that question is obviously in the eye of the beholder. For me, I find inspiration from others I have gotten to know, whether the relationship is personal or professional. The common thread with these individuals is that they possess certain characteristics I admire or have achieved certain goals I wish to achieve. What these individuals are telling me is that what I want is possible. I just have to work for it like they did.

Several years ago I was facing a very challenging time in my life. I was working on some complex issues that were exhausting much of my mental energy. I was also commuting an hour and a half one way while attempting to help my wife plan our wedding ("attempting" being the key word in that sentence). I will never forget the day I felt like I had hit the rock bottom of burnout. I was sitting in my office on a conference call. At the time, my office had a window that overlooked the roof of the floor below the one I was on. There was a contractor out on the roof. He was shoveling rocks after the roof had been replaced. I remember looking at him and thinking how lucky he was to have a job with seemingly little stress. He could just finish the work of his job for the day and not be thinking about it at night. I can remember thinking how envious I was of him. That night as I drove home, I reflected on that guy on the roof and questioned whether I still wanted to do compliance work.

Eventually, I was resolved to the thought that I loved what I did and that I would do it even if I didn't get paid for it. With that said, I realized I needed a boost, something to lift me up. I then started to think about individuals I had known in my life who had inspired me. Those thoughts led to creating a personal board of directors. When I got home, I got out a piece of paper. I drew what looked like an organizational chart, but it was my personal board. There was a board chair and the names of five other individuals I have looked up to, each with certain qualities I strive to emulate.

Having this personal board has helped me countless times over the years. I keep a copy of it in my office today and consult it frequently when I'm faced with a challenging issue. I look up at the names of each board member and reflect upon how they would handle the situation before me. Whatever your source of inspiration is, identify it and consult it frequently. It will serve as a valuable asset to you for navigating the politics of healthcare.

Bonus material: Does the personal board of directors sound interesting to you? If so, go to http://www.bluebirdhealthlaw.com/book-bonuses for a free copy to create your own personal board.

Leverage Resilience During Challenging Times.

The work of a compliance officer is difficult. Whether responding to unexpected issues, navigating political ones, or managing competing high-risk deadlines, each day our ability to stay positive is challenged from multiple angles. A critical component of being professional is being resilient. For the purposes of this discussion, I define "resilience" as the ability to recover from unexpected and difficult challenges. The good news is that resilience is a skill that can be learned if it does not come naturally. In order to ensure your own career longevity, I would encourage you to focus on your resiliency skills. In the spirit of getting you to think about what resiliency looks like for you, let me share an example I draw upon daily: sourcing positive emotions.

What do I mean by sourcing positive emotions? Making a conscious effort to identify and leverage something that evokes a positive feeling. For me, the first one is laughter.

I am a firm believer that laughter is the best medicine. If I've identified that I've not laughed during the day, I intentionally take time out to focus on something that will make me laugh, and the more uncontrollable, the better. Maybe it's a particular show or comedian. Maybe it's talking to an old friend who makes me laugh. If I'm not able to identify a source, my fallback is the infectious laughter of a particular comedian I have stumbled upon.

Another source of positive emotion for me is pride. Ask yourself: What did I do at work today that made me feel proud? Was it tackling a difficult project? Was it finding a compliant solution to green light a leader's business objective? Maybe it was helping a coworker develop a new skill or accomplish a difficult task. If you're struggling to identify a source of pride, set aside time at the end of each day to write down at least one good thing you did that day that made you feel proud. Compliance work is not easy, especially during uncertain times. Developing resiliency skills is a great way to help you adapt to challenging times and effectively navigate the politics of healthcare.

Take Your Work Seriously… but Don't Take Yourself Too Seriously

Without question, compliance work is serious business. The work we do is important to patient care. It is important to the organizations we work for. And it is important to taxpayer-funded healthcare programs. Simply put, the work requires that it be taken seriously. But that does not mean a compliance officer needs to be a serious person…well… not all the time, at least. If you want to effectively navigate the politics of healthcare, take your work seriously, but don't take yourself too seriously.

Now, you may be thinking, "Hey, man. I like a good joke as much as the next person. Are you saying I need to be a comedian?" Not exactly, but let's break this down a little more.

Taking your work seriously means you are passionate about your work. That is true, no matter what line of work you are in—accounting, painting, medicine, plumbing, etc. In the compliance officer profession, there isn't a more accurate indicator of taking your work seriously than passion. Whether it's reviewing regulations or conducting an audit, the work is tedious and labor intensive. As I said earlier, you have to unconditionally love the struggle of compliance work—and that takes a special person to voluntarily endure that kind of pain.

So what do I mean by "Don't take yourself too seriously"? A few thoughts come to mind. First, it means not beating yourself up when you make a mistake. When you are passionate and thorough in the approach to your work, you have the capital to lighten up on yourself. You're human, and all humans make mistakes. As it relates to how you externally process mistakes, of course, you need to take *that* seriously. That is your work. Genuinely apologize and follow through on your steps to correct so that trust is not lost. As it relates to how you internally process the mistake, this is where some people vary in how they respond. You need to be able to laugh at yourself. People who take themselves too seriously become too afraid to fail, and when they do fail, it becomes too much for them to accept. People who are self-confident because they worked hard have no problem admitting their mistakes. They may even bounce back by throwing in a little self-deprecating humor. When you can laugh at yourself in front of others, you are not taking yourself too seriously.

Not taking yourself too seriously also means you have a healthy dose of humility. Now, humility can mean different things, but for me, humility looks like a person who is grateful for what they have. It looks like listening to others and enabling them to be heard. And it looks like asking for help when you need it. These are traits that one should possess, no matter one's socioeconomic background. Let me give you an interesting example of humility that I experienced in my life.

In 1997, I was working as a bartender in Sun Valley, Idaho. Yes, it is true. I was "finding myself" after college. It was a time that my father had *really* hoped wouldn't last long. If you're not familiar with Sun Valley, think Beverly Hills but in the mountains. It's filled with celebrities and the uberwealthy either living or vacationing there. Every day was an out-of-body experience that resulted in me calling my folks to tell them whom I saw. It's a ridiculous fantasyland. A perfect place for someone finding themselves.

At any rate, one night I was working at an annual event put on by a major investment company out of New York. It was a who's who of multimillionaires and multibillionaires. While I was serving drinks before dinner, a gentleman tapped me on the shoulder. He asked me if he could have a glass of wine sitting on the tray I was holding. As I turned around, my twenty-two-year-old male brain mumbled, "Yeah" to this person—but he didn't quite hear me. He said, "Oh. No, I can't have it?" in an almost apologetic tone. As I fully turned around to give him the glass of wine, I immediately recognized who it was. It was Bill Gates. At the time, he was the second wealthiest person in the world, with a net worth of $36 billion.[13] Though I politely replied, "Oh, yes, you can have it," I will tell you inside I was actually thinking, "Holy crap!!! You're Bill Gates! I believe you can have this free glass of house wine!"

I mention this story because I have never forgotten how impressed I was with how he carried himself. It was as if he were no better than I was, though *Forbes* would certainly feel otherwise. Humility is about understanding that we're all equally valuable, and that is demonstrating that you are not taking yourself too seriously.

The takeaway here is that if you want to be effective at navigating the politics of healthcare, take your work seriously but don't take yourself too seriously. This approach can help you in building relationships and communicating with others. Since some healthcare leaders perceive us to be about as impersonal as a computer, this approach can help change the perception of compliance. It adds a human element to your work.

Happiness Comes from Satisfaction

Something I discovered about myself that I did not know when I started my career is that true happiness is the result of feeling satisfied. So it's satisfaction you should be chasing, not happiness. Not to go all *Star Trek* on you, but your career will be a journey through space and time, literally and figuratively. If you think about other journeys you have embarked on in your lifetime, likely there were moments that included a number of emotions: anticipation, excitement, happiness, sadness, stress, fear, and joy, to name a few. In your professional journey, you will experience the same emotions and many more—numerous times over. There will be days you feel you're in complete control and others when you will feel like a rudderless ship out to sea on a course to nowhere. Through all the ups and downs, it's the feeling of satisfaction that maintains the peace within you and keeps you showing up each day.

The concept of chasing satisfaction came to me several years ago after my wife and I bought our first house. As with many couples starting out in their first homes, we bought a fixer upper, which meant lots of home improvement projects. One particular weekend, while my wife was pregnant with our second child, my father-in-law came up to help me work on our son's closet. Now all we did was remove the existing closet hardware and build some new user-friendly shelves. Nothing fancy about it, just a few pieces of wood, cut and assembled, and a fresh coat of paint...and white paint at that. After we finished the project, I can vividly remember how happy it made me feel to reflect on what the closet looked like and see what we did ourselves by hand. I must've had a grin on my face from ear to ear the rest of the day. I remember saying to my father-in-law how happy I was because I could physically see our accomplishment.

It then dawned on me. When I look back on my life so far, it was a sense of satisfaction that came from my accomplishments, big or small, that actually made me happy in life. It wasn't a new car, a nicer house, or a bigger paycheck. Of course those things are nice and can bring happiness, but the feeling is only fleeting. Satisfaction, on the other hand, sustains itself over time and feels as good now as it did in the moment. For me, happiness comes from the satisfaction of completing a project whether it is publishing this book or mowing the lawn.

In your professional life, there are plenty of opportunities for satisfaction. Setting and achieving goals will help in this endeavor. For me, law school was a huge goal. Another one was teaching part-time in academic setting, which I've been doing now for several years. These were goals I set out for myself, which to this day continue to provide me with a feeling of satisfaction in what I have accomplished. They also have continually fueled me to set and achieve new goals.

Satisfaction can also come from tangible things. Earlier I mentioned the home improvement projects. Think about a builder or a painter. If I felt satisfied with a simple closet remodel I worked on, how must a painter feel to drive by a house he or she painted ten years earlier? While we don't paint houses for a living, there are similar opportunities for satisfaction in our line of work: revising a new process to be more effective, implementing a new team-building exercise, or drafting a well written memo. These are just a few examples of opportunities you have available to gain a sense of satisfaction, which can bring you happiness in life.

One final note is that satisfaction doesn't necessarily have to come from things you seek out. In our line of work, satisfaction can also come from resolving difficult and complex issues. You know, the ones that you had no choice but to get involved in, and it's taking months or even years to resolve. As I mentioned earlier, I have found that the most significant growth moments in my career came from times when I resolved the most difficult of issues—these were also moments when I experienced the greatest sense of satisfaction.

Pulling it All Together.

The compliance profession is a practice that takes years to develop. The above thoughts are ones that I did not realize early on in my career but I have come to appreciate over time. These insights are also ones that have kept me engaged to this work, and helped me successfully navigate the politics of healthcare.

Chapter Takeaways

- The compliance profession provides endless opportunities for learning and professional growth.
- Having a big picture approach, being adaptable, and choosing your words wisely will help you in building strong relationships with healthcare leaders.
- You have to unconditionally love the struggle of compliance work if you want to survive in this profession.
- In order to maintain career longevity, find what inspires you, take your work seriously but don't take yourself too seriously, and seek out opportunities for satisfaction.

Conclusion

As we wrap up our time together, I will leave you with some overall thoughts in an effort to pull it all together and identify what your next steps should be.

It's about the *knowing* landscape around you.

Navigating the politics of healthcare is about knowing the political landscape around you. For you, that means knowing which individuals are going to be supporters for the compliance program and which ones are going to be resisters. As I mentioned in this book, there will be some folks who hold formal and informal power in the organization. Your job will be to figure out who these individuals are and whether they are a supporter or a resister. Having this knowledge will help you in determining where you have leverage to advance a particular need of the compliance program's agenda.

It's about *building* strong relationships.

Navigating the politics of healthcare is also about building strong relationships with others. That is true whether we're talking about a supporter or a resister. If you think about having a strong culture of compliance, it truly takes a village of committed folks throughout all levels in the organization in order to pull that off. That means getting others to come to you with concerns proactively instead of reactively. Unfortunately, you can't will such behavior into existence. There are some healthcare leaders, such as the defensive or disengaged ones, with whom you're going to have to work a little harder to gain that trust. If you take the time and put in the effort though to build strong relationships with them, you will experience a payout in a more effective compliance program and a stronger culture of compliance.

It's about knowing *how* to communicate.

Navigating the politics of healthcare is also about knowing how to communicate. That means knowing how to communicate your message in a way that influences behavior, and overcomes times of conflict. When it comes to all the communication strategies discussed in this book, be thinking at least two steps ahead of your audience. What I mean by that is visualize the path forward and identify your next move—before you make the one in front of you. For example, if you are about to communicate with a department director about a topic he or she is pushing back on, assume that director is going to escalate the matter to his or her senior leader. That way before you even communicate with the department director, you'll already be mentally prepared to hear from the senior leader and know how you'll respond. Taking this a step further, if you know the senior leader gives you a leverage point, you may even connect with the senior leader before discussing the matter with the department director.

It's about *staying* neutral in the organization.

Navigating the politics of healthcare is about to maintaining a neutral position in the organization. Remember, the compliance department should function in the organization like Switzerland. In order maintain a neutral position, you need to develop a political strategy that is rooted in productive politics and not destructive politics. Throughout your time in the organization, there will be issues to address and arguments to be made and those will come and go, but relationships must be preserved over time. You may not realize this yet, but it's a small world working in healthcare. If someone leaves the organization, it is likely you will end up working together again at a different one.

Author's Note

At some point every journey must come to an end, and so must ours. I hope this book has been helpful. Considering the relationships a compliance officer has to maintain in order to operate an effective compliance program, the goal of this book was to focus on the work involved in those relationships. In writing this book, I was guided by one overarching question: if I were starting out, what would I want to know?

In response, my focus was not to talk about the Seven Elements or the laws and regulations because those topics have already been covered in other books. Instead, it was to address the business side of healthcare and how to manage some of the key relationships. This is information not really written about, yet it is lived out each day by compliance officers across the country. It's information I wish someone had told me when I started. My hope is that sharing it with you will help make you a successful compliance officer.

Thank you for taking this journey with me. I wish you all the best as you move forward in your own journey.

Jay

Acknowledgments

While my name is on this book, there are so many others who have helped me along the way or assisted in shaping my thoughts over time. Without them, this book would not have been possible. For that reason, I would like to give the following recognition…

First and foremost to my amazing wife, McKenzie. For always believing in me. For pushing me when I didn't want to push myself. Your presence in my life continually challenges my view of what is possible. In so many ways, this book is a reflection of what I have learned from you. Not a day goes by that I don't look at you and think about how lucky I am to have you in my life. I love you so much.

To my daughter, Rubie, and my son, Hill. I don't know what I would do without you in my life. From the days you were born, you both have given my life purpose beyond anything you can ever imagine. My only hope is that one day you will have kids of your own to know exactly how much you mean to me.

To my mother, Jean, and my father, Ed. Thank you for all your love and support over the years. As a parent myself, I've come to know just how much you sacrificed for me when I was a kid. I guess parenthood will do that. Mom, I'm pretty sure the educator in me came from you. Dad, I will never forget tagging along with you on sales calls as a kid. Little did I know at the time that those outings would serve to teach me the importance of building and maintaining strong relationships with other people. This book in many ways is a product of what you both have taught me.

To the members of my personal board of directors: Dan Mulholland, Ruth Krystopolski, Professor David Day, Jennifer Alderfer, Dan Robinson, and Margo Karsten. I guess the cat is out of the bag. You now know that you've been silently mentoring me all these years. I cannot tell you how many times I looked at your names on my board as you helped me through some challenging times. Each of you inspired me to be the kind of professional that I wanted to be. For that, I can't thank you enough.

And to the chairman of that board, the late (Honorable) R. D. Hurd. You will always be the root source of my professional inspiration. I'll never forget the hours we spent walking down the fairway while I was in college, talking about legal careers. I only wish I had the chance to tell you in person how much you inspired me and the promise I made to become a lawyer on the day you died (May 1, 1995).

I also would like to thank Rich Cohan, Diane Gross, and Jennifer Alderfer for reading early versions of this manuscript. I can't thank you enough for your time and insights. Without question, this book benefited from your feedback.

To Ryan Bohy, Kim Patrick, Valerie Clark, Rich Cohan, Stanley Podoloski III, Venetia Marshall, Jennifer Alderfer, Leslie Morgan, Cindy Earnhardt, and David Ledbetter. If you weren't for you, I would not be where I am today, which is a pretty amazing place. Thank you for taking a chance on me.

To Jeff Fitzgerald, Lyn Snow, Mary Crumbaker, Catharine Fortney, Brenda Harstad, Sara Iams, Ranmali Bopitiya, Elizabeth Strammiello, Shawn DeGroot, Margaret Dragon,

Adam Turtletaub, Erika Riethmiller, Kelly McNeil, Andrea McCollough, Christi Belle, Katharine Roberson, Meredith Richardson, Callie Griffith, Elizabeth Carver, Elsie Faciane, Jennifer Sullivan, Megan Zatz, Bob Rowland, Amy Deboer-Kolczak, Matt Weber, Ilene Wolf-Moore, Jeannie Hoover, Judy Hatch, Joanne Davidson, Beth DeLair, Jim Rough, Jan Elezian, Jeff Hyre, Sharon Parsley, Jerry Shafran, and Katie Walter. Words cannot begin to capture how much I valued the conversations and camaraderie we've had over the years. You each have taught me so much for which I am eternally grateful.

I would also like to thank Roy Francia, Katie Dahm, and the editing, production, and design team at Palmetto Publishing. You have made my dream a reality.

Finally, I want to thank you. You don't know this, but we actually spent a lot of time together over a seven-year period as I worked on this book—in my kitchen, in my basement, in my home office, in hotel rooms, at the DMV, and at car dealerships while my oil was being changed. There were even a few nights in front of a fire when I camped with my family and they went to bed early. Countless hours we spent together as I feverishly typed, fictitiously talking to you about information I thought you'd want to hear. You have spent your time and hard-earned money by reading this book, which means more to me than I could ever possibly express to you. Thank you.

A Circle of Life

I'm not sure if it's for you, but if you enjoyed the book and would like to give back, there are two small things you could do for me that would really mean a lot.

#1—Tell a Colleague

If you know a colleague that could benefit from the information contained in the book, please tell them about it. This book has been my attempt to give back to the healthcare compliance community that has given me so much over the years.

#2—Leave a Book Review

If could take a couple minutes today to leave a helpful book review on *Amazon,* I would be grateful. If you've never left a review, and not sure what to say, I'll give you a couple ideas to help get you started:

- You could comment about something you learned from the book.
- You could comment about why you think the book may be helpful to a new compliance officer.

If you want to really help me stand out, leave a 30–60 second video review, or add a photo of you holding the book with your review. Whatever approach you take, just know it doesn't have to be perfect. You can always go back and change it later.

In exchange for taking these small steps, let me know if there is something I can do to support you. Additionally, if I can help answer a question, please don't hesitate to reach out. I can be reached at janstine@bluebirdhealthlaw.com, or you can also reach me on social media.

Bonus Material

Navigating the politics of healthcare is much more than this book. Below are some bonus materials that include information not included in the book.

Book Bonuses.

As I was writing this book, there were times when I wanted to include some supplemental information, but doing so either interrupted the flow of the discussion, or we simply did not have room for it. These are all available to you for FREE. Just go to www.bluebirdhealthlaw.com/book-bonuses.

***Navigating the Politics of Healthcare*: The Blog**

If you want more insights and tips for navigating the politics of healthcare, visit www.bluebirdhealthlaw.com and enter your email address to sign up for my blog.

***Navigating the Politics of Healthcare*: The Course**

If you would like to see the information contained in this book brought to life, I have an online course that will be coming out soon. To receive updates about the course go to www.bluebirdhealthlaw.com and sign up for my email list.

Endnotes

1. *See* "An Open Letter to Healthcare Providers," June Gibbs Brown, Inspector General, February 1997. *See also,* Office of Inspector General, Compliance Guidance, https://oig.hhs.gov/compliance/compliance-guidance/index.asp.

2. *See* Sections 6102 and 6401 of the Patient Protection and Affordable Care Act of 2010 (Pub. L 111-152).

3. *See* 42 U.S.C. §1395nn.

4. *See generally* 42 C.F.R. § 411.357(m). When this exception first became available in 2004, it was $304 per calendar year. This amount is adjusted each year based on the Consumer Price Index and posted on the Centers for Medicare and Medicaid Services website, https://www.cms.gov/Medicare/Fraud-and-Abuse/PhysicianSelfReferral/CPI-U_Updates.

5. *See* 45 C.F.R. Parts 160 and 164.

6. *See* the HIPAA Breach Notification Rule requirements at 45 C.F.R. §§ 164.400-414.

7. The acronym EMTALA is a reference to the Emergency Medical Treatment and Labor Act which can be found at 42 U.S.C. §1395dd. EMTALA generally requires that applicable Medicare participating hospitals and providers ensure public access to emergency services regardless of ability to pay. EMTALA's corresponding regulations found at 42 C.F.R Part 489 further define the applicable hospital and provider's compliance requirements.

8. *See Getting It Done: Experienced Healthcare Leaders Reveal Field-Tested Strategies for Clinical and Financial Success,* Kenneth Cohn (2011), found at: https://www.scribd.com/book/443214706/Getting-It-Done-Experienced-Healthcare-Leaders-Reveal-Field-Tested-Strategies-for-Clinical-and-Financial-Success.

9. *See* K. W. Thomas and R. H. Kilmann, *The Thomas-Kilmann Conflict Mode Instrument* (Mountain View, CA: CPP, Inc., 1974).

10. *See* Jacobellis vs. Ohio, 378 U.S. 184 (1964).

11. Professor Frank Pommersheim (retired), University of South Dakota School of Law.

12. The late Professor John Hageman (USD School of Law)

13. *See* 1997 Billionaire List https://stats.areppim.com/listes/list_billionairesx97xwor.htm.

Printed in the USA
CPSIA information can be obtained
at www.ICGtesting.com
LVHW051947110823
754949LV00038B/1116/J

9 798822 902480